The Basic Photo Book

Phil Davis

Wm. C. Brown Publishers

D1119456

The Basic
Photo Book

Book Team

Editor *Meredith Morgan*
Production Editor *Kay J. Brimeyer*
Designer *K. Wayne Harms*
Art Editor *Mary E. Swift*
Photo Editor *Robin Storm*
Visuals Processor *Joyce E. Watters*

Wm.C. Brown Publishers

President *G. Franklin Lewis*
Vice President, Publisher *Thomas E. Doran*
Vice President, Operations and Production *Beverly Kolz*
National Sales Manager *Virginia Moffat*
Group Sales Manager *Eric Ziegler*
Executive Editor *Edgar J. Laube*
Director of Marketing *Kathy Law Laube*
Marketing Manger *Kathleen Nietzke*
Managing Editor, Production *Colleen A. Yonda*
Manager of Visuals and Design *Faye M. Schilling*
Production Editorial Manager *Julie A. Kennedy*
Production Editorial Manager *Ann Fuerste*
Publishing Services Manager *Karen J. Slaght*

WCB Group

President and Chief Executive Officer *Mark C. Falb*
Chairman of the Board *Wm.C. Brown*

Cover photo © Bob Coyle

ISBN 0-697-11480-5

Printed in the United States of America by
Wm.C. Brown Publishers, 2460 Kerper Boulevard, Dubuque, IA
52001

10 9 8 7 6 5 4 3 2 1

CONTENTS

PREFACE

The photographic image is such a common feature of our cultural environment that it's hard to imagine how we could get along without it. It would be a drab world indeed without photographic illustrations in books, magazines, and newspapers, and without cinema and television; but if we also had to do without scientific and industrial photography the result would be devastating! Industry would slow to a crawl; hospitals would lose many of their diagnostic tools, and scientific research would be crippled. Photography is simply indispensable!

Photography is also an important force in the fine art world and an enormously popular hobby activity that generates literally billions of prints annually and entertains millions of casual "snapshooters." In short, photography touches virtually every aspect of our lives in some way.

If you're a beginner in photography you'll soon discover that unlike the other two-dimensional arts, such as painting, drawing, and printmaking, photography straddles the fence between art and science. Although you are free to choose your subject matter and decide when and how you want to photograph it, your control over the actual process of image formation is significantly limited by the laws of physics and chemistry. Although this makes free expression difficult, it's not impossible; and I think you'll find that the better you understand the fundamental workings of the photographic process the more effectively you'll be able to control it to produce expressive, personally satisfying images. In other words—although it may sound contradictory—becoming a competent technician can help you become a more versatile artist.

In recent years cameras have become so sophisticated that some of them can handle all of the technical details of focus and exposure completely automatically. The simpler, less-expensive cameras of this sort are ideal for casual snapshooters who are interested only in the print results and prefer not to have to bother with the mechanical details.

The more feature-laden and expensive models are popular with professional photographers who often use the automatic functions when they are appropriate, but override them when manual control is preferable.

Although "auto-everything" cameras are convenient to use, and capable enough to handle most ordinary photographic situations, I don't recommend them for beginners. I believe that manual or semi-automatic operation is preferable for school use because these operating modes allow the photographer to decide where to focus and how to set the lens and shutter for best effect. Although automatic cameras can make these decisions for you if you want them to, they reduce the physical act of photographing to an impersonal, mechanical routine.

Of course the selection of subject matter, view point, and light condition allow you some options for creative choice, even with an automatic camera; but manual control of the camera settings offers you additional opportunities to adjust, enhance, and emphasize the important visual qualities of the subject. Just as subtle and appropriate seasoning can make the difference between plain food and a gourmet experience, judicious and sensitive control of the camera settings can often translate an ordinary subject into a memorable image.

Of course, "judicious and sensitive control" suggests that you are familiar with how your camera operates, and that you know what effect each variation of focus, aperture, and shutter speed is likely to have on the image quality. Acquiring this knowledge and skill requires some study and experience, but the learning process can be both exciting and rewarding. If you take it seriously, photography can teach you to see the world around you with greater clarity and enjoyment. It can also provide you with an effective way to express your ideas and emotions, and communicate nonverbally with others.

This book will provide you with the basic knowledge you'll need to make effective, attractive photographs in black-and-white. Although the text does not go into great detail, the essential steps in camera-handling, film exposure and development, printing, and presentation have been included. Numerous photographs are used to support the text and illustrate the various process steps.

The chapters are short and devoted to specific subjects. Technical terms and some other words that may not be familiar in this context are italicized when they first appear in each chapter. For general reference a complete glossary appears at the end of the book.

I hope that you will find the book easy to use and understand, and that it will contribute to your enjoyment of this fascinating medium.

I'd like to thank Phil Auzas and Sarah Tropman for their assistance with some of the illustration material. I'm grateful to Lee Kitada, supervisor of the photographic department of the Home Appliance Mart, for his cooperation in supplying equipment for use in some of the photographs, and to Chuck Eaton, of the Ann Arbor News for facilitating access to their picture files. I also appreciate the technical information and other support provided by technical representatives of the Eastman Kodak Company, the Charles Beseler Company, and the Ilford Photo Corporation.

List of Reviewers

Don Albrecht
Northland College - Ashland

Harold Baldwin
Middle Tennessee State University

David L. DeVries
Califorina State - Fullerton

Gary Pearson
Ricks College

Michael Peven
J W Fulbright College
University of Arkansas - Fayetteville

Authur Okasaki
Tulane University

Neal Rantuoul
Notheastern University

CHAPTER 1

Introduction

Untitled.

Photograph by Kathleen Barrows

This simple, beautifully printed photograph demonstrates the fine sense of composition and awareness of light quality that are typical of Barrows' work.

Figure 1.1
This expensive camera is admired by many professionals, partly because of its modular design which makes it one of the most versatile but also one of the simplest cameras available. The camera body is a metal box to which various interchangeable lenses, film backs, and viewfinders can be attached.

Regardless of its size or complexity, a camera is fundamentally a light-tight box—designed to hold film, equipped with a lens to form the image, and provided with some sort of *viewfinder* to allow the photographer to select and compose the subject area to be photographed, figure 1.1. All but a few small, inexpensive cameras provide some means of *focusing* the lens to form a *sharp* (not blurred) image; and most also allow adjustment of the lens *aperture* and the *shutter speed* so that the film *exposure* (the amount of light that the film receives) can be controlled. Many cameras offer extra adjustments to refine these basic features, and may automate some or all of them, figure 1.2

Photographic films and papers are coated with a light-sensitive *emulsion* of certain silver compounds (*halides*) suspended in a thin layer of gelatin. Suitable exposure to light alters these silver halides to form a *latent* (invisible) image. If the film or paper is then treated in a chemical *developer* solution the latent image becomes visible as the developer gradually reduces the exposed silver halides to minute particles of metallic silver, figure 1.3.

Figure 1.2
This sophisticated camera permits manual control of focus and exposure when that's desired, but it can also be set to operate automatically for "point and shoot" convenience.

Figure 1.3
This print was exposed normally but only that portion of it that's immersed in the developer solution has produced a visible image.

FETY FILM 5062   KODAK

→17A   →18   →1

Figure 1.4
This negative is seen from the back so the image is correctly oriented. The edge perforations indicate that this is 35mm film, the number 18 identifies this frame as the 18th exposure on the film roll, and "5062" identifies the film as Kodak Plus-X.

Because these silver particles are much too small to be seen individually without magnification, they mass together to form the various gray tones of the familiar photographic image. These tones are reversed; that is, the image is dark where it was affected by the light, and remains light in the unexposed areas, so we call the developed film image a *negative,* figure 1.4.

Negatives can be *printed* either by *contact* or by *projection.* When contact printing, or *proofing,* the negatives are pressed firmly against the paper's emulsion-coated surface in a *printing frame* (figure 1.5) or *proofing frame* so the exposing light must pass through the negative silver image to reach the paper. Contact prints are therefore the same size as the negatives from which they were printed.

An *enlarger* is used to produce prints of other sizes by projecting the negative image onto the printing paper, figure 1.6. Prints made this way are generally called *enlargements* but the term *projection prints* is really more appropriate because the print image can be made either larger or smaller than the negative image. Printing a negative by either contact or projection methods produces a *positive* which is really a "negative of the negative," so the tones of the print image resemble the tones of the original subject.

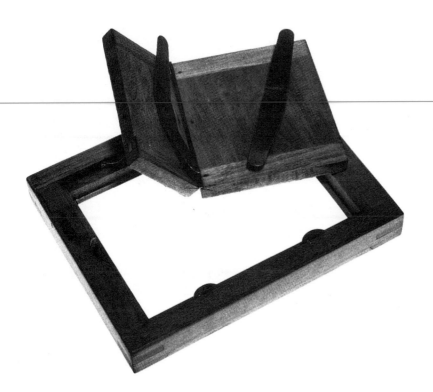

Figure 1.5
This antique printing frame is shown on a light box. In use a negative is placed on the glass, emulsion side up, and covered with a sheet of printing paper, emulsion side down. Then the hinged back is clamped down to press the film and paper tightly together and the exposure is made through the glass.

Figure 1.6
This is a typical enlarger for small roll film negatives. The main unit comprises a lamp housing, a negative carrier, a flexible bellows, and a lens. This assembly can be raised or lowered on the vertical column to adjust the size of the projected image which is formed on the baseboard. Courtesy of the Charles Beseler Company.

Figure 1.7
A mounted print on display.

Prints are usually *mounted* (fastened to a backing board of some sort) or *matted* (positioned in the cut-out opening of an overlaid paper board) for presentation, figure 1.7. If there are visible flaws in the print image they should be *spotted* (painted or bleached out) before the print is displayed.

2

Hints for Photographing Effectively

Watching the Parade, Chicago.

Photograph by David Alan Jay

Jay's informal "street photograph" invites the viewer to answer the question
"Who are these people and what's going on here?"

You don't have to be an art critic to know that some photographs are more interesting than others. The question is, "why?" Subject matter is obviously part of a photograph's appeal but there's more to it than that. As you gain experience I think you'll discover that *what* you photograph isn't critically important—it's *how* you do it that counts.

If there were a "best" way to photograph things, making good pictures would simply be a matter of following the rules. Fortunately, that isn't the case. Artistically, at least, you're free to photograph anything that interests you in any way you like—but even deciding what's worth photographing can be a problem.

It may help to consider why you're interested in photography at all. Do you especially enjoy the *activity* of photography (looking for subject matter, using the camera, working in the darkroom), or are you mainly interested in the resulting photographs as *objects* to be shared with friends, exhibited, or sold? Are you attracted to photographs that depict things accurately and objectively, or do you prefer images that are more abstract or ambiguous? Do you favor pictures of people, or pictures of things or places? Does the spontaneous, informal quality of snapshots appeal to you, or would you rather look at more finely crafted, more formally composed images?

There isn't any best answer to questions such as these, but they should prompt answers of some sort. It's important for you to have opinions or convictions because photography is an essentially neutral medium that doesn't have any opinions of its own. If your photographs are going to "say" anything, you'll have to supply the ideas and make sure they're properly expressed.

Of course, photography is not verbal so photographs don't ever "say" anything in the same way that words do. At best they can only present visual symbols or metaphors that sensitive viewers may be able to interpret.

How can you make interesting photographs? Rules have no place in art but there are a few guidelines that are generally worth considering. First, photograph what genuinely interests you, and try to express your interest in visual terms because the camera can record only what it can "see." It can't respond to other sensations (sounds, odors, tactile qualities) that may be part of your perception, so you'll have to translate these nonvisual perceptions into visual metaphors if you want them included in your work. Don't rely entirely on subject content, either; photographs of interesting situations or objects are not *necessarily* interesting pictures!

Simplify and clarify your concepts. Try to place the camera so that the important elements of your picture are emphasized, and nonessentials or distracting elements—especially in the background--are subdued or eliminated, figures 2.1-4 . In general, it should be fairly apparent what a photograph is supposed to show or "say," but remember, a photograph is more than just a description of the

Figure 2.1
The point of this appealing snapshot--a little girl teasing her mother--is weakened by the background foot that appears to be attached to her head. The glaring white of the sock emphasizes the problem. Background interference of this sort is common in these informal situations and you'll have to be very alert and quick to avoid it.

Figure 2.2
This soaring figure is cleanly outlined against a clear sky and a high shutter speed has frozen the action so that the visual structure of the photograph is clear. What is the boy doing, and why? That's for each viewer to decide. Photograph by Phil Auzas.

Figure 2.3
This view of a carved stone figure illustrates its relationship to the town below but is visually confusing because the tone and textures of object and background are fairly similar.

Figure 2.4
The same figure seen from a lower viewpoint is now silhouetted against a pure white sky, and can be examined without background interference. The relatively great exposure that was required to preserve detail in the shadowed areas of the figure has "burnt out" the details of the buildings below. Although the faint images of the buildings continue to establish the relationship between the figure and the town, the emphasis is now clearly on the figure.

Figure 2.5
The subject of this photograph is not particularly important at first glance because of the extremely rich texture and elegant forms. In this case much of the charm of the image is due to its visual quality--what it represents is less important than what it looks like.

subject; it is also an abstract pattern of visual elements arranged in a well-defined space. That pattern arrangement—the composition of the image—can be just as important as the subject itself, figure 2.5. If the subject seems to be uncomfortably proportioned or awkwardly placed in the print format, viewers are likely to find the photograph irritating rather than attractive, even though they may not know why, figures 2.6,8.

Figure 2.6
How do you photograph a concept or feeling such as "swinging?" This attempt is obviously ineffective. Although it does describe the situation well enough, and a slow shutter speed has introduced some motion blur, the emphasis is wrong and the background is obtrusive.

Figure 2.7
A higher shutter speed has stopped the action and only the little girl's apprehensive expression and tightly clenched grip on the rope suggest that the swing is actually moving. The older girl's black-and-white striped costume competes for attention as does her stare at the camera.

It's not easy to *over*simplify a photograph, but it is possible. Be sure that you don't eliminate so much that the image is pointless and sterile. Although good composition is certainly important, it's only the skeleton of a picture; most photographs need more than simple structure or pattern effects to be interesting for more than a few moments, figures 2.9,11.

Figure 2.8
This is more like swinging! "Panning" (swinging the camera to follow the motion) and a slow shutter speed have blurred the background while keeping the figure quite sharp. The background streaks and the girl's blowing skirt and hair all suggest rapid motion, and her ecstatic expression completes the picture. Almost every element in the photograph contributes to the statement that swinging is fun.

Figure 2.9
This bold pattern of dark and light shapes forms an arresting composition but its appeal is largely visual. The large figure 7 is both an attractive graphic shape and a provocative symbol that suggests some unexplained meaning. Cover up the 7 or imagine the picture without it and see how the image emphasis changes. What does it mean? That's for the viewer to decide.

Figure 2.10
The arched structure of the canopy over this pedestrian overpass forms a rich visual pattern that's enhanced in this view by the cast shadows. Some viewers will find its simple symmetry boring, others may be distracted by the distorted landscape forms seen through the windows. Is this subject worth photographing? You decide.

Figure 2.11
The same overpass, photographed from a slightly different viewpoint and in late evening light. The confusion of outside elements has been reduced, the shapes simplified, and the canopy structure is even more graphic. The flaring light at the end of the walkway is now an important visual element, and it's apparent that the changed light condition has altered the mood of the picture. The interpretations are obviously different; which do you prefer?

Add a little magic if you can, figure 2.12. Photography is fundamentally a copying medium that tends to describe things in minute detail. This is a desirable characteristic if you're interested in simple documentation but it makes free expression difficult. If you want your images to be interpreted poetically, or seen as metaphors rather than simply as pictures of things, be sure to leave something to the viewer's imagination. Things taken out of context, unusual juxtaposition of objects, distortions of any sort, or any other provocative or ambiguous elements in your photographs are all likely to attract the viewer's attention and invite his or her participation,

figures 2.13,15. Although individual interpretations may vary considerably, people are likely to be favorably impressed by images that challenge their imaginations.

Finally, do whatever you choose to do as well as you can. Familiarize yourself with all of your camera's features and learn to use them intuitively. Investigate the characteristics of your materials—film,

Figure 2.12
This photograph was obviously inspired by the dramatic light effect but the man's figure provides an element of mystery. Some viewers will enjoy this image for its graphic appeal, some may see it as a poetic metaphor, while others may interpret it literally and wonder what's happening and why the man is standing there. How do you prefer to read it? Photograph by Phil Auzas.

Figure 2.13
What have we here? Is this a many-legged freak, a road-kill, a metaphor for protest or pain, or just an old cat yawning and stretching in the sun? This technically-poor (underexposed) photograph has made the cat's form indistinguishable from her shadow and isolated her gaping mouth in a shapeless black void. These distortions invite fanciful interpretation but the literal rendering of the cat's extended foot and the recognizable texture of the carpet tend to dispel the mystery. What's your opinion?

Figure 2.14
This photograph seems to be a simple record photograph of a sleeping puppy and you have probably imagined a situation that explains where he is and why he's tired. But the puppy might be dead; does that affect your impression?

Figure 2.15
This photograph shows the puppy from a different perspective and gives you some more elements to deal with. How can you explain the patch of light and the little doll in the upper left corner? How do they relate to the puppy? If you are interested in either of these photographs which do you prefer?

developer, and printing paper–and learn the techniques and craft of developing and printing so that you can exert real control over the image quality, figures 2.16-17. Then be sure your prints are properly finished before presenting them.

If you photograph thoughtlessly, without much passion, or blunder around carelessly in the darkroom, your lack of interest will almost surely show in your prints. You can hardly expect viewers to take your work any more seriously than you do yourself!

Figure 2.16
This photograph of a tortured old tree is realistic and descriptive of its appearance in soft morning light.

Figure 2.17
In this photograph a strong red filter has darkened the sky and the image has been "printed down" (darkened) a little to emphasize the highlights on the branches. Although this is a distortion of reality, some viewers may prefer this dramatic effect to the more literal rendering above. This illustrates only one of many techniques you can use to emphasize those elements of your subjects that you consider to be important. Learn as much as you can about your equipment and materials so that you can use them creatively.

Figure 2.18
Children are attractive subjects but not all photoghaphs of children have universal appeal. This photograph by news photographer John Heider is one of the "rejects" from a series he did for a feature story on a T–Ball league. Although this picture would almost certainly be appreciated and enjoyed by this boy's friends and family, it's not likely to impress strangers. Even some people who know the boy may be put off by the awkward foreshortening of his arms and the ambiguity of his gesture in this photograph. Although it is possible to determine that he's about to throw a ball, it's not immediately clear and the action is not well explained visually. Courtesy of the Ann Arbor News.

Despite your best efforts you may be disappointed by other people's response to some of your photographs. There are at least two good and related reasons for this. First, photographs in general are no longer news; we're so accustomed to seeing photographic images in newspapers and magazines, on billboards, in the theater, and on television, that they've become almost invisible. Second, your view of your own work is certain to be influenced by "wishful seeing," and your photographs may not actually be what you think they are, figures 2.18,19. The features that seem so obvious and interesting to you may

Figure 2.19
An instant later the throw has obviously gone astray and this photograph speaks in universal body language. Anyone who has ever made a mistake will recognize and sympathize with this gesture which clearly says "OOPS!" To capture the essence of situations like this—Henri Cartier–Bresson called them "decisive moments"—you'll need quick reflexes because timing is critical. Photograph by John Heider, courtesy of the Ann Arbor News.

not be obvious at all to other viewers. Without knowing what they're supposed to see, they can respond only to what is actually displayed. Unless something attracts their attention immediately they may simply see your work as "more photographs," and move along without examining the images carefully.

If your critics have missed your message or failed to appreciate the features of your work that you consider to be important, try to find out what they think the pictures *do* illustrate or express. They may have overlooked or misunderstood some symbol or metaphor, or may have been distracted by some unimportant detail or some technical flaw. Their feedback can help you see your own work more objectively, and help you produce more effective images in the future.

Of course, some people will not agree with your choice of subject matter or your image style, but that simply reflects a difference in taste and should be expected. It's healthy to acknowledge these differences but try not to let them influence you unduly. After all, art is a personal matter and your work is yours alone; no one else can know what you like, how you think, or what you feel.

You can learn a great deal by discussing your (and others') photographs, and the opinions of more experienced photographers can help you recognize weaknesses in your work. But it's also important to trust your own instincts. If you enjoy the activity of photographing, if your work reflects a sensitive personal taste, and if you work hard at improving your technical skills, it's very likely that, sooner or later, other people will begin to enjoy your photographs, too.

3

Camera Types and Features

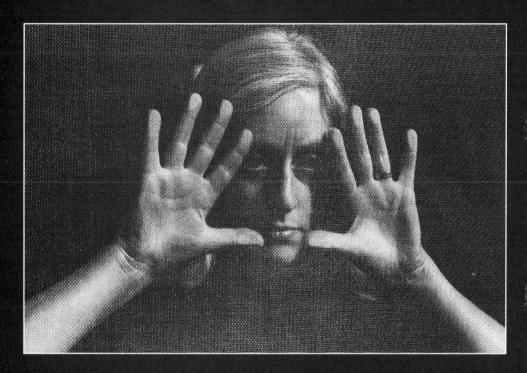

Untitled.
Photograph by Jean – Claude Lejeune

Figure 3.1
A disposable camera.

Figure 3.2
Relatively inexpensive cameras of this sort are excellent for beginners because they provide all the necessary features, there's little to go wrong with them, and their manual controls are easy to use.

In an apparent effort to appeal to the casual "snapshooter" some manufacturers have marketed disposable cameras, figure 3.1. Designed for just one use, each of these cameras comes preloaded with film and is equipped with a lens, shutter, and viewfinder of the simplest sort.

Although these "throwaway" cameras can produce pictures of fairly good quality when conditions are favorable, the cameras that most photographers prefer are more highly-refined machines, figures 3.2, 3, 4. For example, the camera *body,* may be precisely cast and machined from aluminum or some other metal, or molded from some

Figure 3.3
Semi-automatic cameras such as this feature more versatile exposure metering systems, dedicated electronic flash capability, and semi-automatic exposure control, but film advance and focusing are manual.

Figure 3.4
Although these more advanced cameras permit some degree of manual control, they're capable of fully automatic operation. With that versatility comes design complexity, relatively high cost, increased size and weight, and total dependency on battery power. This model is equipped with an interchangeable autofocus zoom lens.

lightweight but durable space-age plastic material. The film-handling mechanism may load and advance the film automatically. The lens may be a carefully-assembled composite of several individual glass elements, and may *zoom* to cover a wide range of *focal lengths*. It may also focus automatically. The shutter may be able to measure time intervals as long as 30 seconds or more, or as short as 1/2000th second, or less. The *viewfinder* will certainly provide a clear view of the intended subject area and may also include a *focusing aid* such as a *micro-prism grid* or a *rangefinder prism* (see figure 4.8).

Virtually all *small-format* cameras and *medium-format* cameras feature built-in *exposure meters*. The meter measures the subject light, then calculates settings of the lens *aperture* and *shutter* that will provide proper exposure for the film. If the meter is designed to operate in automatic or *programmed* mode, it will set the lens and shutter controls automatically. In *semi-automatic* mode it calculates the settings and allows you to select either a lens (*aperture priority*) or shutter (*shutter priority*) setting, after which the camera will set the other value for you.

In *single-lens reflex* (SLR) design the meter is generally incorporated into the viewfinder, and exposure (and other) information is displayed in the margins of the viewfinder window.

In addition, many modern cameras will accept a wide variety of lenses which can be interchanged quickly and easily at any time. Some cameras are equipped with built-in *motor drives* that advance the film after each exposure, and are capable of exposing several *frames* per second, automatically, for sequence photography. In some designs the motor may also load the film, then rewind it back into its protective *cartridge* when the last frame has been exposed.

Many popular cameras are designed to accept accessory *electronic flash* units for use when the subject light is dim. Miniature electronic flash units are built into some camera bodies and are designed to turn themselves on and fire automatically when they sense that the subject requires the extra light, figure 3.5.

As you can see, the trend is toward more automation and greater design complexity and some cameras are so "intelligent" that they hardly need a human photographer at all! But we are not yet entirely obsolete; cameras can handle the mechanical aspects of picture-making, but they can't make aesthetic decisions.

In fact, the camera's automatic settings may not always result in the "best" picture. Sometimes you may want to photograph a subject out-of-focus, or use motion blur for expressive effect. You may want to alter the normal tonal scale of the image occasionally, by deliberately over- or underexposing the film. Although the popular "point and shoot" cameras make this sort of control difficult, most other cameras will let you override their automatic features and take command.

Figure 3.5
"Point-and-Shoot" cameras typically have built-in electronic flash units. These very popular cameras are small, light, relatively inexpensive, and fully automatic—and they usually make remarkably good pictures. No manual control is possible so they're not a good choice for student use.

Button

Socket

Figure 3.6a
Shutter release: Press this button to release the shutter and make the exposure. In some cameras you must press the shutter release button lightly to activate the exposure meter or illuminate the shutter speed scale in the viewfinder.

Figure 3.6b
Cable release socket: You can screw a cable release into this socket and use it, instead of the button, to release the shutter.

It's a good idea to put the camera on a tripod and use a cable release for exposure times greater than about 1/30th second—especially when using lenses of longer-than-normal focal length.

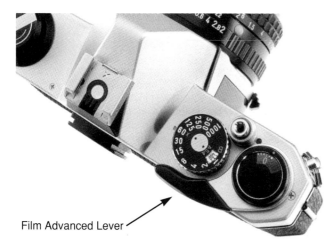

Film Advanced Lever

Figure 3.6c
Film advance lever: Swing this lever after each exposure to advance the film and "cock" the shutter. This lever is missing from Point-and-Shoot cameras, and from many automated SLRs, because they contain tiny motors that advance the film after each exposure.

Shutter
Speed Dial

.Figure 3.6d
Shutter speed dial: On this camera the shutter speeds can be set by turning this ring, but they will not be operative unless the meter switch is set to the "manual" position. This shutter speed ring is unusual; most cameras provide a knob for setting manual speeds, and it is frequently combined with the ISO film speed setting dial. "Point-and-shoot" cameras set the shutter speeds automatically and don't provide for manual control.

Film Speed
Setting

Figure 3.6e
Film speed setting: This camera combines the film speed setting dial with the exposure "override" control. Set the ISO speed of the film you're using into this window and leave the override dial set at 0 for normal operation. "Point-and-shoot" cameras, and many other automated models, don't provide this manual control because they "read" the film speed from a printed code on the film cartridge and adjust the meter automatically.

Flash Shoe

Figure 3.6f
Flash shoe: An electronic flash unit can be mounted directly in this "shoe." Some cameras may not have this feature. Others may have "dedicated" flash shoes featuring extra electrical contacts that allow the camera to control the flash duration, and provide in the viewfinder a visual indication of the flash readiness and effectiveness.

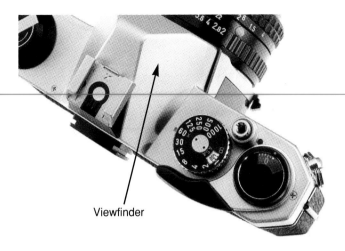

Viewfinder

Figure 3.6g
Viewfinder: This "pentaprism" finder is a distinguishing feature of SLR (single-lens reflex) cameras. It provides an erect, laterally correct image of the subject area as seen through the camera lens. Most cameras also display information about the exposure settings and other camera controls in the margins of the image area. All modern cameras provide some focusing aid, such as a "microprism grid" or a "rangefinder prism" (or both) in the center of the viewfinder image area.

Rewind Knob

Figure 3.6h
Rewind knob/Back latch: Use this knob or crank to rewind the film into the cartridge after you have exposed all of the film. Be sure to press the film release button before attempting this. If the film has not been released it may tear if you try to rewind it . Many cameras now combine the rewind knob with the camera back latch; to open the back, pull up firmly on the rewind knob. Cameras that include motorized film transport don't have a rewind crank so a separate back latch is provided.

Lens Assembly

Figure 3.6i
The lens assembly, including the focusing and aperture controls, is interchangeable.

Focusing Control Ring

Figure 3.6j
Focusing control ring: Turn this ring to focus the image. The subject distance in feet and meters is indicated on the footage scale, opposite an index mark on the lens body.

Depth of Field Scale

Figure 3.6k
Depth of field scale: This scale is used in conjunction with the focusing control to estimate the distance between the nearest and farthest points of satisfactorily sharp focus in the subject area.

Aperture Control Ring

Figure 3.6l
Aperture control ring: Turning this ring adjusts the aperture size. The selected f-number is indicated on the aperture scale, opposite an index mark on the lens body.

Lens Lock

Figure 3.6m
Lens lock: Depress this button while
turning the lens body to remove the lens
from the camera.

Flash Socket

Flash Socket

Figure 3.6n
Flash socket: Although the flash shoe
provides a convenient method of holding
a flash unit and triggering the flash when
the shutter opens, it's also possible to
operate a flash unit at some distance
from the camera by plugging it into this
socket.

Film Release Button

Tripod Socket

Figure 3.6o
Film release (rewind) button: Press this button to release the film so that it can be rewound into the cartridge before you open the camera back. On some cameras this button may be located on the top of the camera body or, instead of a button, it may be a lever located on the front of the camera body. On automated cameras a similar button not only releases the film but also switches on a motor that rewinds the exposed film.

Figure 3.6p
Tripod socket: Used to mount the camera on a tripod.

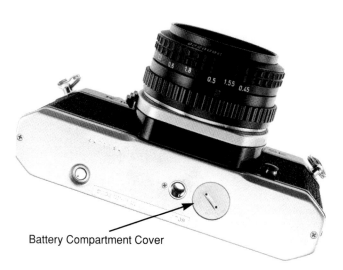

Battery Compartment Cover

Figure 3.6q
Battery compartment cover: Remove this cover to inspect or change the batteries. A coin such as a penny or a quarter can be used as a "screwdriver." Automated or motorized cameras usually use larger batteries that may be housed in the built-in hand grip.

Caring for Your Camera

Figure 3.7a
Clean the inside of your camera frequently. Blow dust out of the film chamber and off of the mirror with a rubber syringe. *Don't* touch the mirror surface; it is very fragile and easily damaged.

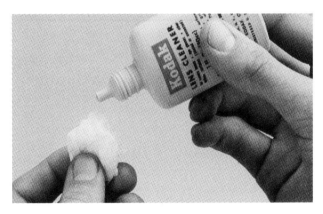

Figure 3.7b
Don't clean the lens surfaces unless they are obviously dusty or soiled; then begin by dusting the glass very gently with a soft brush to remove loose particles that might scratch the glass during cleaning.

Figure 3.7c
Alternatively, blow off the surface dust with a rubber syringe. Don't use "canned air!" Although public concern about ozone depletion has finally forced the manufacturers to stop selling Freon as "air," the safety of their substitute gases has not yet been fully established.

Figure 3.7d
Moisten a clean, crumpled piece of lens tissue or a clean ball of surgical cotton with a drop of lens cleaning fluid . . .

Figure 3.7e
. . . and rub the lens gently with a circular motion until the soil is loosened. Then polish the surface dry with a fresh piece of lens tissue, crumpled into a soft wad, or a clean ball of surgical cotton. Be gentle!

4

Viewing, Framing, and Focusing

Chauncey.

Photograph by Kathleen Barrows

Barrows makes unpretentious photographs of things that matter to her,
and does them with tasteful elegance. Her interest in the qualities of
texture and light are evident here.

When you look into your camera's viewfinder (or "finder") you get a preview of the scene that the camera will record. If your camera is an SLR the viewfinder image is formed by the *taking lens* itself, figure 4.1. Cameras other than SLRs view the subject through a separate optical finder system, figure 4.2. The image they display may be framed and proportioned correctly but it's not exactly the same image that will be recorded on film.

Both viewfinder types have their advantages: the SLR finder *groundglass* image shows the out-of-focus portions as blurred, just as they'll appear in the final print, so you can focus and check the *depth of field* visually (by pressing the *preview* button). It also shows you how foreground objects relate to their backgrounds and displays correct image perspective. On the other hand, the SLR finder image is relatively hard to see clearly in dim light, or at small apertures, and it blacks out completely while the shutter is open. This is usually only a minor inconvenience, but it makes photographing rapidly moving objects a little uncertain. Of course, an SLR finder is totally useless during *time exposures.*

Figure 4.1
In single-lens reflex cameras the subject light enters the "taking" lens and is reflected upward by an inclined mirror to a groundglass screen. This single reflection produces an image that is right-side-up but laterally reversed. This image then undergoes further corrective reflections inside a glass pentaprism, and is finally presented to the eye correctly oriented. In this design the camera lens forms both the viewfinder image and the final film image, so "what you see is what you get."

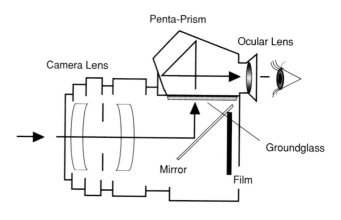

Figure 4.2
Small cameras that are not SLRs must rely on separate viewfinders to find and compose the image.

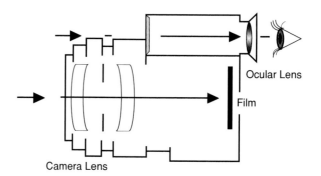

The separate optical viewfinder, used by most point-and-shoot cameras, is relatively bright and easy to use in dim light and is unaffected by the shutter action, so moving objects are easy to follow and photograph. On the other hand, it provides no information about depth of field; and framing and composing the image are less precise because the finder and the camera lens "see" the subject from slightly different viewpoints, figures 4.3,4. This *parallax error* is generally insignificant at normal subject distances but can be a problem when you work at very close ranges.

Most viewfinders *crop* the image somewhat—that is, they don't show quite as much of the subject area as the film will record. The SLR image is generally more precisely defined than the image you'll see in the usual point-and-shoot finder, but with either type you can be reasonably sure that everything you see will also appear in the photograph, with a little room to spare. For this reason it's normally safe (and desirable) to compose your subject tightly so that it fills the whole image frame.

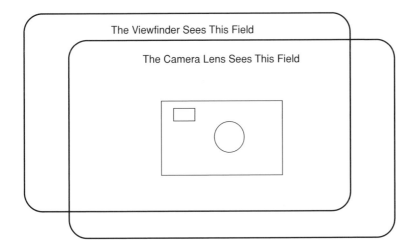

Figure 4.3
Since the viewfinder "sees" the subject from a point of view that's slightly displaced from the lens axis, there is some parallax error—that is, the lens and finder fields are slightly displaced ...

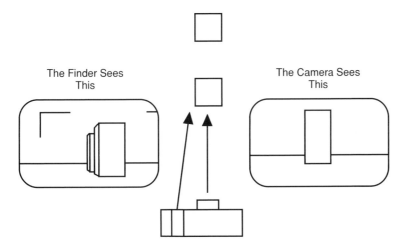

Figure 4.4
... and 3-dimensional subjects are seen and photographed in slightly different spatial relationships. The effect is exaggerated in this illustration, and is generally of no real consequence at subject distances of more than a few feet; but at closer distances it can be bothersome.

Figure 4.5
This is the sort of information that advanced automated cameras may display in the margins of the viewfinder. Symbols of this kind can indicate what mode (manual or automatic) the camera is operating in, whether the exposure override control is in use or not, whether the flash unit is ready to fire and, after firing, whether or not the exposure was sufficient, whether the meter is operating in spot, averaging, or some other mode, or whether the autofocus mechanism has been able to focus satisfactorily. Some cameras will supply less information than this; others may provide more.

Figure 4.6
This screen display is typical of that found in relatively inexpensive point-and-shoot cameras. The symbols in the lower margin indicate the general subject distances that the camera's autofocus mechanism can adjust for. The symbol in the screen center marks the subject area that the camera will consider in determining the focus distance. The outer frame line defines the boundaries of the subject area that will be included in the picture when the lens is focused on distant objects. The short angled line in the upper left corner of the image area defines the approximate boundary of the subject area that will be included at the shortest focus distance—a graphic reminder of the effect of parallax at close range.

You will probably see some numbers, symbols or lines in the viewfinder window, either superimposed over the groundglass image area itself or arranged in the border area around the image. Most SLRs display at least the basic exposure settings—the *f-number* and *shutter speed* currently in use—and some provide a great deal more information, figure 4.5. Point-and-shoot cameras are usually less informative because most of their functions are totally automatic. There may be some marks in the finder area to indicate the image boundaries for closeup work (to counteract the parallax error) and there will probably be some symbol indicating the focusing "target" area, figure 4.6.

Figure 4.7
This is typical of the screen display you're likely to find in basic "no-frills" SLRs. The circular rangefinder prisms occupy the center of the screen, surrounded by a micro-prism grid (which is really much less obtrusive than this illustration indicates). Exposure is adjusted manually by changing the settings of either the aperture or the shutter—or both. Normal exposure is indicated when the needle is centered in the gap, as shown here. Overexposure is indicated when the needle swings toward the "+" sign. The "-" sign warns of underexposure.

Figure 4.8a
The SLR viewing screen contains a diagonally divided rangefinder prism, surrounded by a circular micro-prism grid, and a ring of fine-textured groundglass for visual focusing. The rest of the screen area is a Fresnel lens whose concentric line pattern shows in the corners of this detail. The camera is focused on the crest of the snow-covered hill in the middle distance; the building corner is slightly out-of-focus.

Although some SLRs provide automatic focusing, most still require manual adjustment of the focusing control and include one or more *focusing aids* such as a *micro-prism grid* or a *rangefinder prism* in the center of the viewfinder window, figure 4.7 . These devices are designed to emphasize the out-of-focus effect; the micro-prism grid fractures the image so that it shimmers when the camera is moved slightly, and the rangefinder prism splits the image and displaces the halves. Focusing the lens eliminates or minimizes the shimmer and aligns the split image halves so that the image appears quite normal, figure 4.8.

Figure 4.8b
When the camera is focused for close-up, both the building corner and the hill are out-of-focus.

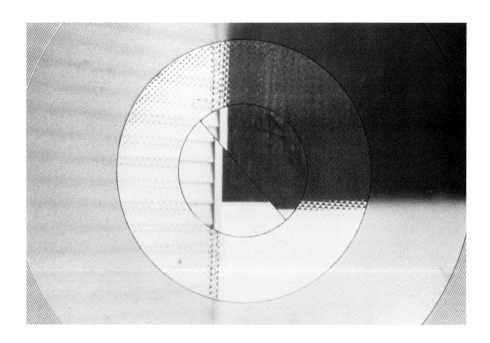

Figure 4.8c
Stopping the lens down renders both focusing aids useless and the groundglass grain shows strongly.

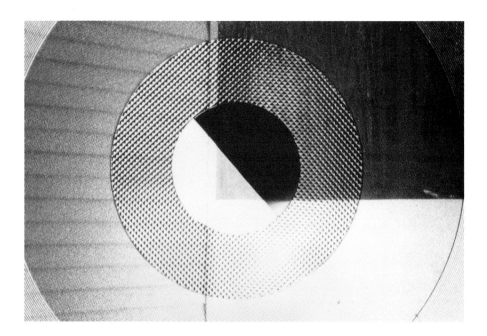

Both of these focusing aids work best with lenses of approximately normal *focal length*, used at maximum aperture. When used with extreme *wide-angle* or *telephoto* lenses, or when the lens is *stopped down* to a small aperture, the normal micro-prism grid simply appears granular and one-half of the rangefinder prism turns completely black. The groundglass area surrounding the focusing aids continues to function properly, however, so you can still focus the camera in the usual way by adjusting the focusing control until the image appears to be sharp.

All contemporary SLR viewfinders include a special screen of some sort to provide a brilliant, evenly-illuminated viewfinder image. *Fresnel lenses*, which can be identified by their overall pattern of fine, concentric circular lines, have been used for this purpose for many years. They are still common, but many cameras now employ equally effective, unobtrusive screens of more modern design.

Autofocus cameras work either by "measuring" the distance to the subject with an infrared or ultrasonic beam or by "analyzing" the sharpness of some portion of the image itself. In both cases the measured or sampled area of the subject is small and generally located in or near the center of the subject area (see figures 4.5 and 4.6). Since it's sometimes desirable to place the most important subject area off-center in the image frame, most of these cameras provide a "focus lock" of some sort. This allows you to focus normally by centering the subject and pressing the shutter release lightly. This light pressure on the shutter release locks the focus adjustment so that you can swing the camera as necessary to recompose. Then depress the shutter release the rest of the way to take the picture.

Although autofocus mechanisms are good, they're not infallible. The infrared (IR) or ultrasonic (US) types can't focus through windows or focus on mirror images, and other types can be fooled by subject areas of uniform tone, pattern, or texture. On the other hand, the IR and US types can focus in total darkness, and the more advanced models of both types can often adjust the lens more rapidly and more precisely than is possible manually.

5
CHAPTER

Lens Types and Features

Untitled, Guatemala, 1991.

Photograph by Janice Levy

Levy is a "street photographer" who favors wide-angle lenses
and likes to photograph people at very close range.
Her images are often ambiguous and many have symbolic content
that is left to the viewer to interpret.

Figure 5.1
(Normal lens diagram) Modern camera lenses are complex assemblies. The shape, thickness, and polish of each glass element—and the spaces between elements—are all precisely controlled.

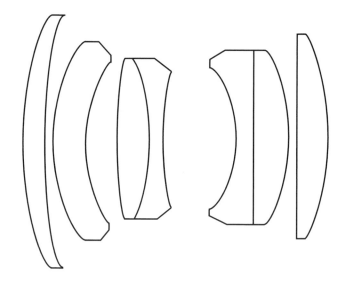

Figure 5.2
This picture of the interior of an old church was taken directly against the light from a high window. Although the window was well outside the picture area and its light was diffused, it was sufficiently bright to cause this flare effect. A good lens shade would have protected the lens and minimized this problem.

Your camera lens is really a magnifying glass—but a very sophisticated one. It almost certainly contains three or more simple lenses, mounted either singly or cemented together, in two or more groups, figure 5.1. This complex assembly is neccessary to correct the inherent *aberrations* (functional defects) that prevent simple lenses from forming images of high precision.

The surfaces of most of these glass elements are *coated* to reduce internal reflections and flare, figures 5.2,3, and improve image contrast. It's this coating that gives the lens surfaces their characteristic purplish or amber glint.

When you turn the focusing ring on your camera lens you'll notice that the lens moves toward or away from the film and that the distance between lens and film diminishes as the lens is focused on more distant objects. There are limits, of course: most ordinary cameras can't move far enough forward to focus on an object thats less than

Figure 5.3
When a bright, direct light source is actually in the picture area, both general flare and flare spots like these are likely to appear. Because some of the flare light may be reflected back and forth between the lens elements several times before it reaches the film, some flare spots are brighter and some larger than others. All of them are images of the opening in the lens diaphragm, however, and because this diaphragm has 6 leaves, these spots are all hexagonal.

about 16 or 18 inches from the lens. On the other extreme the lens is as close to the film as it can get when it's focused on a subject that's a few hundred feet away. Beyond this distance, which is generally greater for large cameras than for small ones, no futher focusing adjustment is necessary.

At this *infinity* focus setting the distance between (an optical measuring point in) the lens and film is called the focal length. This is a fixed "dimension" of the lens that's determined by the shape and arrangement on the lens elements themselves. It's important because it's related to image size—lenses of long focal length produce larger images than "short" lenses can. Also, it affects light transmission or *lens*

Figure 5.4
The markings on this lens include the lens type (Zuiko Auto-S), the focal length (50mm), the relative aperture (1:1.4), the serial number (1130697), and the country of manufacture (Japan). The relative aperture describes the *maximum* aperture; that is, when the diaphragm is fully open.

speed, so that a long lens is "slower" (transmits less light to the film) than a lens of shorter focal length—if their aperture diameters are the same.

For convenience we use this relationship (focal length divided by aperture diameter) to identify and compare the speeds of different lenses or different aperture settings. For example, if the focal length of a lens is 8 inches and it's diameter is 2 inches, the *relative aperture* (the ratio of diameter to focal length) is 1:4. You'll probably find the relative aperture of your lens marked on the lens barrel or on the retaining ring that holds the front element in place, figure 5.4. Typical values for 35mm SLRs are 1:1.4 or 1:1.8. Point-and-shoot camera lenses are usually slower and may be marked as 1:2.8 or 1:3.5.

Although manufacturers use these ratios to identify lens speeds, photographers don't. We almost invariably use *f-numbers* which simply replace the "1" in the ratio with "f/" so that, for example, 1:1.4 becomes f/1.4 and 1:2.8 becomes f/2.8 (spoken as "eff two eight"). This merely reverses the relationship by stating that the aperture (diameter) is equivalent to the focal length (f) divided by the ratio number.

The aperture scale on your camera lens is calibrated in a standard series of these f-numbers that will probably include 2, 2.8, 4, 5.6, 8, 11, and 16. Notice that the series can be extended in both directions by doubling (or halving) every second number. For example, the number following 16 is 22 (twice 11), the next 32 (twice 16), and the number preceding 2 is 1.4 (half of 2.8).

Each of these numbers identifies a specific aperture and we refer to them as *stops* because each setting of the aperture "stops" a certain percentage of the subject light from entering the camera, figure 5.5. Each larger f-number in the standard series transmits just half as much light as the preceding one; for example, f/16 transmits half as much light as f/11, and f/4 transmits twice as much light (is twice as "fast") as f/5.6. In changing from one aperture setting to a smaller we "stop down;" but we "open up" from a smaller aperture to a larger one.

1.4   2   2.8   4

5.6   8   11   16

Figure 5.5
Each of these f-numbers, or f-stops, identifies a particular lens opening. Each number, therefore, stands for a specific amount of light transmission through the lens. The series is calculated so that changing the aperture setting from one f-stop to the next higher one (from f/2 to f/2.8, for example) will halve the light intensity that reaches the film. The lens aperture's capacity for light transmission is commonly referred to as its *speed*, so in the example above, we'd say that f/2 is *faster* than f/2.8 (actually twice as fast). Notice that as the f-numbers increase, their speed decreases; thus, for example, f/16 represents a very small opening and is very much *slower* than f/1.4. Set the aperture control on its fastest speed (largest opening, smallest number), then look into your lens and notice that the diaphragm is fully open. Watch the opening as you turn the aperture control ring to its smallest stop. If your camera is *not* an SLR , you'll see the diaphragm close as the ring is turned. If the camera *is* an SLR, the lens will probably remain wide open, regardless of the aperture setting. This is normal; SLR lenses are designed to stay open to maintain the brightest possible viewfinder image until the instant of exposure. Then, as you press the shutter release, the diaphragm automatically stops down to the aperture you've preselected and the shutter opens to make the exposure. As soon as the shutter has closed, the diaphragm snaps open again.

Figure 5.6

Figure 5.7

Figure 5.6
A popular point-and-shoot camera with its zoom lens retracted to provide its shortest focal length of 38mm.

Figure 5.7
Here the zoom lens is extended to its full 90mm focal length. The markings on this lens include the term "macro-zoom," indicating that the normal focusing range of the lens can be extended to permit "closeup" photography.

Because each stop changes the exposure by a factor of 2x, we frequently express exposure changes of any sort in stops; for instance we might say that a film of ISO 400 speed is "2 stops (meaning 4-times) faster" than ISO 100, or describe a shutter speed setting of 1/60th second as being "a stop slower" than (half as fast as) 1/125th—even though neither of these examples has anything to do with the lens aperture.

Cameras generally come equipped with lenses of "normal" focal length, which implies that the lens focal length is approximately equal to the diagonal measurement of the camera's image rectangle. This should mean that the normal focal length for 35mm cameras (whose image dimensions are about 24 x 36 millimeters) is about 43mm, but the popular 35mm single-lens reflex (SLR) cameras are exceptions to this rule: they normally come with 50mm (focal length) lenses. This focal length number is generally marked on the lens mount or retaining ring and may be identified by a lower-case "f," for example, "f = 50mm."

Point-and-shoot cameras generally have 35 to 45mm lenses and some models include *telephoto converters* that can nearly double the normal focal length when a longer lens is desired. A few models offer real *zoom* lenses that provide continuously-variable focal length, figures 5.6, 7. Most SLR cameras allow the normal lens to be removed easily and replaced by a lens of different type, such as a telephoto or *wide-angle* lens.

The main advantage of a telephoto lens is that it provides a relatively magnified view of the subject (a disadvantage is that it also magnifies the subject or camera movement). On the other extreme, a wide-angle lens can reduce the image scale to include much more of the subject area than is possible with a normal lens from the same vantage point, figure 5.8a, b, c.

In general the "coverage" of a lens is (approximately) inversely related to its focal length. For example, if your normal 50mm lens can include a 20-foot-wide expanse of some subject, a 25mm wide-angle lens will record about 40 feet of the subject's width, and a 100mm lens, from the same position, will let you select a 10-foot section and fill the frame with it.

Figure 5.8a
The 24mm wide-angle lens used for this photograph covers an angular horizontal field of about 72° which has included a wide expanse of seascape as well as Ramon's sign.

Figure 5.8b
The normal 50mm lens covers a horizontal field of about 38° and, when used from the same position, produces a more normal-looking view that includes only the center portion of the scene.

Figure 5.8c
A 100mm telephoto lens, used from the same spot, cuts the scene width approximately in half again to provide a relatively magnified view of the shed. Since the camera position was unchanged for this series, the image *perspective* is identical in all three photographs. Only the area covered has changed.

Figure 5.9a
In this photograph the camera was positioned about 20 feet from the steps. The ruined temple in the background is about 1/4 mile away. A 24mm lens was used to make the picture.

Figure 5.9b
The normal 50mm lens, used at a distance of about 40 feet, keeps the steps about the same size but alters the perspective. The distant ruin is now pictured in what appears to be its normal scale, relative to the steps and the people.

Figure 5.9c
Moving the camera back to about 80 feet from the steps, and equipping it with a 100mm telephoto lens, produced this photograph. The scale of the steps is approximately the same but now the subject space seems compressed and both the people on the steps and the background ruin loom unnaturally large.

If you use lenses of different focal length at different subject distances, adjusting the distances so that the image size remains the same, the image perspective will appear to change and the size relationship between foreground and background objects will be affected noticeably, figure 5.9a, b, c.

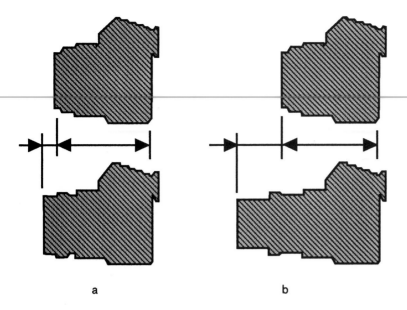

Figure 5.10
When focused on infinity regular lenses and macro lenses of the same (50mm) focal length extend a similar distance from the camera body. Their focusing mounts are quite different, however; the general-purpose lens (a) can be extended only far enough to focus sharply on objects about 16 to 18 inches away, but the greater extension of the macro lens (b) allows it to focus down to about 9 inches.

a   b

Zoom lenses are even more versatile. Although lenses of fixed focal length are generally smaller, lighter in weight, and faster than zoom lenses, and may be capable of slightly better image quality, the ability to adjust image magnification makes zoom lenses very appealing. This is particularly true when you need to compose carefully in the full image frame as, for example, when shooting color slides that will be viewed by projection.

By comparison with the limited focusing range of ordinary lenses, *macro* lenses are capable of focusing on objects at any distance from infinity to just a few inches in front of the camera, figure 5.10. At their closest focusing distance they typically produce images that are about one-half lifesize, but when used with an accessory *extension tube* or *bellows* unit, some can photograph subject details that are recorded at lifesize on the negative. Macro lenses are specially designed for maximum efficiency at these short ranges, and most are of approximately "normal" focal length.

Some f/2.8 macro lenses are available but apertures of f/3.5 or f/4 are more typical. These special lenses can't compete with "normal" lenses for sheer speed but their image quality is typically excellent and some photographers prefer them to more conventional high-speed lenses for general work.

If you don't need the slightly greater sharpness and convenience that the macros provide at close range, you can make *closeups* of satisfactory quality by fitting a relatively inexpensive supplementary "closeup lens" over your normal lens. Closeup lenses are simple, high quality *positive* lenses that are usually supplied in threaded mounting rings, just as filters are, so they can be screwed directly into the threaded front flange of your lens.

These supplementary lenses are usually marked in *diopters*—that is, the reciprocal of the focal length in meters. For example, a +1 diopter lens has a focal length of 1 meter, or about 40 inches; a +2 diopter lens has a focal length of 1/2 meter, or about 20 inches, and a +3 lens has a focal length of 1/3 meter, or about 13 inches, and so on.

Figure 5.11a
This flower was photographed with a normal 50mm lens, set at its closest focusing distance of about 17 inches (measured from the subject to the plane of the film). The image width has been cropped slightly but the full height of the negative image is represented.

Figure 5.11b
With a +1 supplementary lens affixed to the lens, with the focus setting unchanged at 17 inches, the subject distance was reduced to about 14 inches and this image resulted.

When a closeup lens is added to the camera lens, the camera's new focusing range begins at a distance equivalent to the focal length of the closeup lens, and decreases as the focusing ring is turned, figure 5.11a, b, c, d. This is how it works:

Camera lens focused at:	Infinity	10 ft.	3 ft.
+1 lens shifts focus to about:	40"	30"	20"
+2 lens shifts focus to about:	24"	20"	16"
+3 lens shifts focus to about:	17"	15"	13"

Figure 5.11c
The +2 supplementary lens, used under the same conditions, permitted this photograph to be made at a subject distance of about 12 inches.

Figure 5.11d
When the two supplementary lenses were used together to produce a total power of +3 diopters the subject distance was reduced to a little less than 11 inches. Combining lenses like this tends to reduce image sharpness, which may offset the advantage of the increased magnification. Macro lenses will generally produce better image quality than this at these very close ranges.

These distances are approximate and are measured from the film plane; the actual subject distances measured from the front of the lens mount will typically be about 3 inches less than these.

An SLR equipped with either a macro lens or a supplementary lens is very appropriate for closeup work, but choose the macro for best image quality. If you use a camera that does not permit through-the-lens (TTL) viewing and metering, closeup work is haphazard at best and supplementary lenses are your only practical choice.

CHAPTER 6

Film Types and Features

Untitled.

Photograph by Jean–Claude Lejeune

Films come in a wide variety of sizes and types. The most common size is generally referred to as "35 millimeter" (because it's a 35mm-wide strip) but its official designation is "135." It's generally packaged in disposable metal *cartridges,* usually in lengths of 24 and 36 exposures. The manufacturers identify their various film types by printing bar-codes and bold geometric light and dark patterns (called DX codes) on each cartridge, figure 6.1. Professional photo-finishing machines can scan the bar-codes to identify the film type and provide the proper processing conditions, and many modern cameras read the DX codes for film speed and other information and adjust the camera controls appropriately.

Originally this film size was intended for use in motion picture cameras (which explains its perforated edges) but the Leica camera, that was designed to use it in 1927, was so enormously popular that other manufacturers quickly followed suit with designs of their own and 35mm film became a standard.

The popular "full frame" 35mm image area is a rectangle about 1" high by 1 1/2" long, or about 24 x 36 millimeters. The less-common "half frame" cameras produce images that are about 1" high by 3/4" wide. Other 35mm formats are relatively rare.

The most common *rollfilm* size is designated as "120." It also provides several format sizes, the most popular being 4.5 x 6 cm (about 1 5/8 x 2 1/4 inches), 6 x 6 cm (about 2 1/4 inches square) and 6 x 7 cm (about 2 1/4 x 2 3/4 inches).

Basically, film consists of a light-sensitive *emulsion* of gelatin and silver compounds, coated thinly on an acetate or mylar plastic base. The emulsion itself is usually a creamy gray, tan, or pink color but a colored *anti-halation* coating is usually applied to the back of the film base. This coating is typically blue, green, or brown, depending on the film type. Its function is to absorb light that passes completely through the emulsion so that it can't be reflected back to cause blurry "halos" around the image highlights.

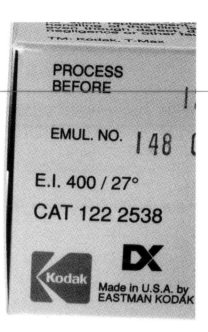

Figure 6.2
The procedure for testing film sensitivity and assigning film speed numbers is specified in publications by the American National Standards Institute (ANSI) and the International Standards Organization (ISO). The "official" film speed values, so found, are identified by the prefix "ISO," and combine both American (arithmetic) and European (logarithmic) numbers; as, for example, ISO 40 0/27 . The logarithmic number, identified by the " ° " sign, is not meaningful for American photographers, so we usually ignore it and say simply "ISO 400." Despite this accepted standard, it's not uncommon to see film speeds defined as "E.I." (for Exposure Index) numbers. This suggests that the speed number has been assigned by some procedure other than the official one—perhaps to indicate an effective speed that can be obtained by nonstandard film processing techniques.

To reduce halation still further, and to minimize *light piping,* the plastic base material that is used for 35mm films also contains a gray dye. Because this gray plastic base is only a few thousandths of an inch thick, its density has no effect on image quality and merely requires a moderate increase in printing exposure. But light that strikes the edge of the exposed film *tongue* (that usually protrudes from a 35mm cartridge) and might ordinarily be "piped" through several inches of clear film base, is strongly absorbed by the dye and prevented from entering the cartridge to *fog* the film.

Films are very sensitive to light. Because film exposure must be closely controlled for best results, we need to know how sensitive a particular film is in order to adjust the camera controls appropriately. The film's *ISO speed* rating (the term that has replaced the older *ASA rating*) gives us that information. It's worth noting that manufacturers (and individual photographers) sometimes recommend speed numbers that are not based on the ISO standard, but are considered to be practical for some purposes. These " unofficial" speed numbers are properly referred to as *Exposure Index* or *EI* numbers.

The ISO film speed numbers are printed on some film cartridges, most film packages, and on the instruction sheets that are sometimes included, figure 6.2. The numbers indicate film sensitivity directly; for example, a film rated at 100 is just half as sensitive—and will therefore require just twice as much exposure—as a film whose speed rating is 200.

The gray tones of a photographic negative appear to be smooth and textureless but they are actually composed of masses of minute silver particles that, under some magnification, give the image a granular appearance, figure 6.3a,b,c. In general, "fast" films form

Figure 6.3a
The grain structure of the film negative is apparent in these 22-diameter enlargements. By examining the sign image you can see that this film of moderate speed (ISO 100) produces very fine grain (which may not be visible at all in reproduction).

Figure 6.3b
This medium-fast film, rated at ISO 400 by its manufacturer, forms a noticeably grainy image.

Figure 6.3c
This high speed film, with a manufacturer's rating of E.I. 3200, is distinctly grainy but the overall image quality is still quite acceptable.

Figure 6.4

Figure 6.5

grainier, less sharp images than slow films do; so for best image quality under good light conditions, a slow film (ISO 100 or less) is probably the best choice. Choose a medium-speed film (ISO between 100 and 400) for general use, and reserve the high speed films (ISO over 400) for action shots in dim light, or for those situations where emphasized image grain is desirable for an expressive or graphic effect.

Although a simple silver emulsion is sensitive mainly to blue light—and not extremely sensitive even to that—most films are coated with refined *panchromatic* (or "pan") emulsion types that respond to all of the colors of the visible spectrum as well as invisible ultraviolet (UV) radiation. However, even though a panchromatic film can respond to colored light, it can't reproduce the subject's colors as colors; they're represented in the negative image as shades of gray, figure 6.4.

Orthochromatic (or "ortho") films are also sensitive to UV, blue and green but not to red light. They are not generally available in the popular rollfilm sizes but are widely used in the graphic arts and other specialized areas.

Figure 6.4
We perceive color in the subject as having hue (red, green, etc.), intensity or value (lightness or darkness), and saturation or purity. Our popular general-purpose black-and-white films are designed to record these colors as shades of gray.

Figure 6.5
This translation isn't always satisfactory when the original colors are different in hue but similar in intensity; but in most instances the print results are acceptable.

Figure 6.6a
If you're a beginner I suggest that you use a medium-speed black-and-white film such as KODAK Plus-X, KODAK T-MAX 100 (TMX) or Ilford FP-4, and plan to work in good daylight. If you prefer to work in color, try a *color slide* film such as KODAK EKTACHROME 100. Avoid bright light while loading or unloading your camera. On this typical camera the back latch is released by pulling up on the rewind knob.

Figure 6.6b
Be sure the inside of the camera is clean and dust-free. Insert the film cartridge, then push the rewind knob down to engage the cartridge spool.

Figure 6.6c
Insert the film tongue into the slotted take-up spool and be sure it's fully engaged and straight. Some photographers prefer to do this before inserting the cartridge into the camera.

Figure 6.6d
Wind the film by working the advance lever and releasing the shutter until both rows of perforations are mated with the teeth of the sprocket wheels. Then take up the slack film in the cartridge gently by turning the rewind knob until the film is under slight tension. Don't overdo this or you may cause *cinch marks*--short horizontal scratches--on the film. Close the camera back and wind off two exposures to get rid of the exposed film *leader*.

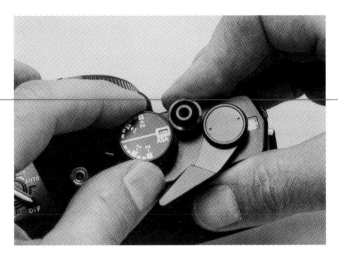

Figure 6.6e
If your camera cannot read the DX film speed code from the film cartridge, or if you're using a film that is not DX coded, set the film speed manually now before you forget it.

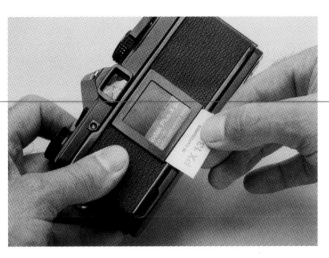

Figure 6.6f
If your camera is equipped with a reminder frame of this sort, insert the end flap from the film box in it so you won't forget what kind of film you have in the camera.

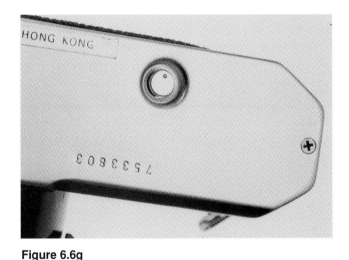

Figure 6.6g
After exposing all the pictures on a roll of 35mm film, you must rewind the film into its original metal cartridge before it's safe to open the camera in the light. To do this you'll have to release the film sprocket wheel by flipping a lever, turning a knob, or pressing a button on the base plate. Then turn the rewind crank or knob until you feel the film leader (or *tongue*) pull loose from the take-up spool and reenter the cartridge. It's then safe to open the camera and remove the film cartridge.

7 CHAPTER

Meters and Metering

Untitled.

Photograph by Jim Shaffer

Proper film exposure involves four factors: the sensitivity (or speed) of the film; the brightness (or *luminance*) of the subject; the lens opening or aperture (f-number); and the exposure duration (shutter speed).

The *ISO film speed* number is listed on the film box and is also provided as a bar-code on 35mm cartridges (see figures 6.1 and 6.2). Some SLRs, and all point-and-shoot cameras, can read the film speed from this cartridge bar-code and adjust themselves automatically, but other cameras require that the film speed number be set manually in a window or on a dial on the camera body.

However it's accomplished, the camera's built-in *exposure meter* must "know" how much light the film needs before it measures the subject's luminance and adjusts (or recommends adjustment of) the aperture and shutter speed controls.

Measuring the subject luminance would be simple if the subject were a uniform tone and color, figure 7.1, but most real subjects contain areas of light and dark tone, as well as textures of various sorts,

Figure 7.1
Meters must recommend a specific exposure so they must necessarily calculate an average value of scene luminance, despite the fact that individual luminance values of the various subject areas will usually vary over a wide range. In other words, the meter doesn't see the extremes of luminance, it bases its exposure recommendation on the assumption that the subject is a more or less uniform shade of gray. In this case the subject luminance *is* quite uniform, and approximates a middle gray, so the meter handles it easily.

figure 7.2. Most camera meters average these tones to arrive at some medium value and adjust the lens aperture and shutter speed to expose that "middle gray" value properly. Then areas of a normal subject that are darker than middle gray are effectively underexposed and are rendered dark in the print (or slide); and light areas are effectively overexposed and rendered light in the final image—which is exactly what should happen.

However, if you photograph the same scene with two different cameras you may discover that their meter readings don't agree. That may be because the meters are averaging the scene's luminances differently. A few meters consider all areas of the scene to be equally important and provide an overall average value. The more common *center-weighted* meters assume that the center area of the subject is most important, and pay relatively little attention to luminance values that appear near the edges and corners of the image area, figure 7.3.

Figure 7.2
The average luminance value of this more typical subject is difficult to calculate because the relatively small statue is intensely bright while the much larger area of shade and shadow is generally dark. Not all meters will agree when appraising subjects of this sort.

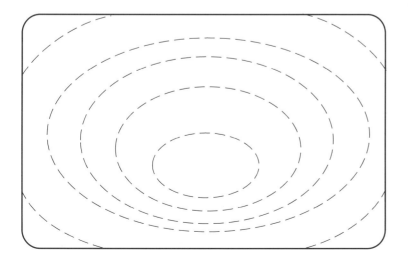

Figure 7.3
This diagram is an idealized example of the sensitivity pattern of a center-weighted meter. The small oval area in the center represents the region of greatest sensitivity. This suggests that any subject luminance that falls within that area will be given great "weight" when the various luminances are averaged. Sensitivity decreases progressively toward the margins of the image field so that the luminance values of details that occupy the extreme corners of the field may be virtually ignored. Many meters—but not all—assign the greatest weight to the lower center of the image area, as indicated here.

Figure 7.4
Some modern automated cameras use a degree of "computer intelligence" to compare the luminance values in several well-defined areas of the image field before calculating an average value. In some cases the central circular area can be selected separately and used for making spot readings of individual subject areas.

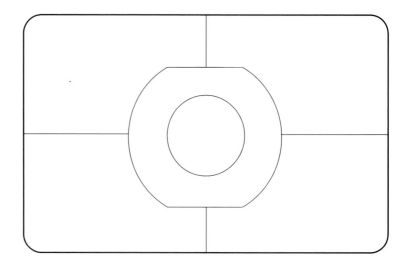

Figure 7.5
Adjust the override control on your camera to help the meter cope with subjects that are abnormally light or dark in tonality. Don't think of this adjustment as simple exposure compensation—that would suggest that light subjects should be given less exposure and dark subjects given more. In fact, that's exactly what the meter will do if you *don't* correct it. The override control simply allows you to "tell" the meter, "your normal decision will not interpret the subject the way I'd like it, so do it *my* way!"

Some meters divide the field into a number of specific areas of sensitivity, figure 7.4. Others may provide optional *semi-spot* readings, each of which is restricted to a relatively small, generally well-defined area of the image field. This feature is especially valuable for use with abnormally light or dark subjects, because it allows you to measure small areas of specific subject tones for the meter to consider in arriving at its average value.

Regardless of the method used, all meters calculate exposure settings that are appropriate for "normal" subjects. But all subjects are not "normal." Some are mostly light in tone so that their average value is abnormally light, others have abnormally dark average value. In both cases, though, the meter assumes that you want the average value to be middle gray, and adjusts the camera accordingly. This tends to underexpose the light subject and overexpose the dark subject.

You can correct for this tendency by adjusting the camera's *override* control, figure 7.5. As a general rule, setting the override control at "+2" (2 stops overexposure) will expose a near-white subject well, and

Figure 7.7
Setting the override control at +2 "overexposed" the white subject enough to make it print more realistically. Although this might be called a bad exposure, technically, it's appropriate and desirable here.

"+1" (1 stop over) is likely to be satisfactory for a subject of overall light tone, figures 7.6, 7. Try "-2" if the subject is near-black overall, and "-1" if its average appears to be very dark gray, figures 7.8, 9. If the picture is important it's wise to *bracket* the exposure—that is, make one correct exposure, then one that's overexposed by 1 stop, and another that's underexposed by 1 stop. For example, if you feel that "-1" is the correct adjustment for some dark-toned subject, make another exposure with no override correction (1 stop overexposed), and an additional one at the "-2" setting (1 stop underexposed). One of these three negatives is likely to be good even if you have miscalculated slightly.

Figure 7.8
This black factory building doorway was in deep shade but the meter attempted to "correct" it to middle gray by recommending a substantial increase in exposure. The result suggests a gray building in hazy sunlight. This a "good" exposure, but an unrealistic interpretation of the scene.

Figure 7.9
This image resulted from setting the override control on -2. This version of the image may or may not be preferable, aesthetically, but it matches the visual appearance of the scene closely.

Recognizing subjects that require override compensation will take some practice. Subjects seen in silhouette against bright backgrounds or against an actual light source are particularly difficult to appraise because, even though most of the subject may be nearly black, a small area of very bright light may fool the meter into "thinking" that the overall average value is lighter than it appears to be, figure 7.10.

Study the subject first and try to visualize its average value; remember that the meter will attempt to record the average as middle gray. Then consider how you want to interpret the subject. Again,

remember that if you don't override the meter it will tend to record predominantly light subjects as darker than they appear, and predominantly dark subjects as lighter than they appear. Finally, after using your override control, be sure to return it to normal so that you won't continue to "correct" future pictures inadvertently.

CHAPTER

8

Depth of Field

Self Portrait, Antigua, Guatemala, 1991.

Photograph by Janice Levy

Photographic self–portraits are not uncommon but Levy's complex deep–space composition and masterful control of image gradation give this one unusual appeal.

Figure 8.1
When this 50mm lens is focused on 10 feet and used at an aperture of f/8 the depth of field is indicated to be between about 7 3/4 and 14 1/2 feet. These scales make it easy to see how the depth is affected by the aperture setting; for example, if you were to stop this lens down to f/16, without changing the focus, the depth of field would extend from about 6 1/3 feet to about 25 feet.

If you examine the focusing ring on your camera's lens you'll see that it includes a *footage* (or *distance scale*) that indicates the approximate distance to the point of sharpest focus in the subject. If it is not a zoom lens there will also be a *depth of field scale* consisting of several pairs of f-numbers straddling the focusing index mark.

Turn the focusing ring to set the focus distance at 10 feet then check the distances that are aligned with the two "f/8s"—one on either side of the focusing index mark. On this lens those distances are about 7 3/4 and 14 1/2 feet, figure 8.1. This means that if you have set the lens aperture at f/8 and have focused sharply on something that's 10 feet from the camera, the *depth of field*—or region of satisfactorily sharp focus in the subject area—will extend from 7 3/4 feet to 14 1/2 feet.

Now, without changing the focus setting, check the depth of field for f/2 and f/16. Notice that the smaller aperture (f/16) provides much greater depth of field (extending from about 6 1/3 to about 25 feet, in this case) and the larger aperture (f/2) provides much less—from about 9 1/2 to 10 3/4 feet.

Practically, this means that if you want everything from foreground to background to be as sharp as possible, you should use a small aperture—perhaps the smallest one your lens provides. On the other hand, if you want some specific section of your subject to be in sharp focus, and don't mind some out-of-focus blurring in the foreground and background, you can use a large aperture to minimize the depth of field, figure 8.2.

The depth of field scale can help make that aperture choice. For example, if you're photographing a baseball game and want to prepare for some action at some particular point in the field, focus on the near side of the area you want to cover, then on the far side, and note both

Figure 8.2
This owl was photographed from a distance of about
11 1/2 feet with a 250mm lens. At its maximum aperture of
f/5.6, the depth of field extended from only about 11 feet to
about 12 feet—enough to render the owl's plumage
clearly, but the branch extending toward the camera and
the trees in the background are far out of focus.

Figure 8.3
Using a 300mm lens to get close to the action in this T-ball game, news photographer John Heider prefocused to include this zone of potential excitement and waited. A high shutter speed has stopped this youngster in mid-stride as he winds up to gun the ball toward first base. The large aperture has narrowed the depth of field to just a few feet and reduced background confusion to a minimum. Courtesy of the Ann Arbor News.

distances. Then set the focusing ring on your lens so that those two distances straddle the central index mark and are aligned with similar f-numbers on the aperture reference scale. The camera will then be focused most sharply on the distance indicated opposite the central index mark, but the entire area you've selected will be satisfactorily sharp, figure 8.3.

This focusing method—setting the lens so that everything between two selected limits will be in focus—is called *zone focusing*.

If you examine the distance markings on the depth of field scale you'll discover that the depth increases as the subject moves away from the camera until eventually the scale indicates *infinity*. Beyond this point everything is equally sharp and no further focusing is required.

Figure 8.4
Focusing any lens on infinity insures that things in the distance will be sharp but the nearest plane of sharp focus may not be as close to the camera as you'd like it to be. In this case the near plane appears to be at about 24 feet.

Figure 8.5
Adjusting the focus to place the infinity mark on the scale opposite the chosen aperture (f/11 in this case) moves the near plane of the depth of field closer to the camera. Notice that the camera is now focused most sharply on about 24 feet, and the near plane is now about 12 feet. The near plane distance when the lens is focused on infinity is called the "hyperfocal distance." When the camera is focused on the hyperfocal distance, the near plane is located at half the hyperfocal distance and the far plane extends to infinity.

It might appear that you can provide for the greatest possible depth of field by setting the focus on the infinity mark. For example , if you choose to work at an aperture of f/11 and set the scale on infinity you'll find that the near plane of acceptable sharpness lies at about 24 feet but that the far plane extends well beyond the infinity mark, figure 8.4.

That's a considerable range but you can do even better than that. Readjust the focusing ring so that the *far limit* of the depth of field falls on infinity and you'll see that the range is now even greater—in this case, from about 12 feet to infinity, figure 8.5. This focusing method—

setting the far limit on infinity—is called *hyperfocal focusing,* and provides the greatest depth of field that's possible for any given aperture setting.

Because there isn't room on the depth of field scales to include all of the f-numbers, or very many distance markings, you'll have to estimate the intermediate values and the information is not very precise, figure 8.6. If you're not sure of the exact settings, it 's generally best to use the nearest marked settings that will provide greater depth.

There are several factors that influence depth of field but the three most important ones are the aperture, the focal length, and the subject distance. As a general rule, small apertures provide greater depth than large apertures do; short focal length lenses provide greater depth than long (focal length) lenses do, and depth of field increases as the subject distance increases.

Therefore, for maximum depth, choose the shortest lens you have, stop it down as far as it will go, and set the footage scale for hyperfocal focusing, figure 8.7. For minimum depth, use a long lens, open the aperture to maximum size (lowest f-number), get as close to the subject as possible, and focus sharply on the subject area you're interested in, figure 8.8. If you follow this advice you'll quickly discover that there may be a practical limit to your control, because some of the factors that tend to increase depth of field also tend to reduce the image size, and vice versa. In general you'll probably decide that some compromise is best.

Finally, when control of depth of field is not particularly important—and when the light conditions permit it—it's a good idea to choose some mid-range f-number because either very large or very small apertures may reduce image sharpness slightly.

Figure 8.7
The depth of field scale of this short (24mm) focal length lens, used at f/16 and 'hyperfocal focused,' indicated that the near plane would fall about 2 1/2 feet from the camera. In this picture the nearest fence post was about 3 feet from the lens. Both it and the distant horizon are satisfactorily sharp.

Figure 8.8
On the other extreme, in making this photograph of a "jack-in-the-pulpit" a 100mm lens, used at its shortest range (about 3 feet) and set at its maximum aperture of f/2.8, produced a depth of field of only about 1 inch. That was sufficient to record "Jack" sharply, but the front edge of the "pulpit" is unsharp and the background clutter of leaves and twigs has dissolved into a blur of soft grays.

9

Light

Untitled.

Photograph by Kathleen Barrows

Stripping photography almost to its barest essentials,
Barrows created this dramatic photograph
in which the subject is "light."

a

b

The fact that we can't make photographs without sufficient light is obvious enough but good photographers also realize that the *quality* of light is even more important than its intensity.

Light direction, for example, affects the rendering of form and texture, influences contrast, and contributes significantly to the "mood" of a photograph. *Front light*—that is, light that strikes the subject from the direction of the camera—minimizes contrast and texture and tends to make the subject look two-dimensional, figure 9.1a. *Cross light,* from the side or top of the subject, emphasizes form and texture, and increases contrast, figures 9.1b, c, d. *Back light* tends to silhouette the subject, reducing both form and texture, figure 9.1e.

The *area* of the light source determines whether the light will be *soft* or *hard.* Large area sources, such as an overcast sky or a reflecting wall surface, tend to produce soft, gentle light that reduces contrast, figure 9.1b. A smaller-area source such as an ordinary light bulb used in a small reflector, produces less-diffused light that casts relatively well-defined, dark shadows and increases contrast, figure 9.1c.

If the light source is close to the subject it will tend to illuminate the subject unevenly, producing a harsh, glaring, visual effect, figure 9.1d. Distant sources illuminate the subject much less harshly but tend to produce distinct, sharp-edged shadows that may be distracting, figure 9.1f.

If there is more than one light source, and especially if they are of similar intensity, the separate sets of highlights and shadows that they produce is likely to be confusing and unattractive, figure 9.1g. This is partly because we use highlight and shadow information intuitively in visualizing the 3-dimensional form of the pictured objects. Multiple light sources present us with conflicting clues about form and surface and hinder our interpretation.

In many photographic situations you will not have much control over the source (or sources) of light but you can often move either the subject or the camera, or both, to make the best use of the existing

c

d

Figure 9.1c
When the area of the light source is reduced (in this case by replacing the large floodlamp reflector with a smaller one) the illumination is "harder" and contrast is increased. For some purposes this sort of interpretation may be preferable to a softer, more subtle one.

Figure 9.1d
Moving the light source close to the subject increases contrast dramatically. The "burnt out" highlights and black, textureless shadows, produce a harsh, glaring effect that is quite irritating.

e

f

Figure 9.1e
Back light turns the subject into a flat, black shape without texture, detail, or gradation.

Figure 9.1f
When the small-area light source used in figure 9.1c is moved farther away from the subject the shadow areas are much more sharply defined but gradation is relatively subtle and there is none of the glaring harshness that results when the light is too close, figure 9d.

g

Figure 9.1g
When two light sources of approximately equal strength illuminate the subject from opposite sides, the highlight and shadow patterns formed by each light are canceled by the other. As a result there are no real highlights and the sense of 3-dimensional form is greatly reduced. When this sort of lighting is used for portraiture—a common beginners' mistake—the effect is especially unpleasant.

Figure 9.2
If this picture had been made directly toward the window the little girl's figure would have been shown in total silhouette and might have blended confusingly into the other forms. By moving the camera to take advantage of some cross light, it was possible to capture her rapt expression as she watches the floating balloon, while emphasizing the expressive gesture of her hands.

light conditions, figures 9.2, 3—or postpone the shot until the light changes, figures 9.4a, b. These decisions won't be easy at first, because you've probably spent most of your life so far learning to see and recognize things *regardless* of light conditions.

The problem is that we don't see things as the camera will record them. Our eyes aren't designed to see large areas sharply. We build up an impression of a scene by a whole series of quick glances at the details, treating each tiny area more or less separately. Although we do get a general overall feeling for the total area from our wide peripheral vision, we never get the single, fixed, detailed, visual description of the scene that the camera lens will form.

Figure 9.3
A high vantage point for the camera and low, direct sunlight combine to shift the emphasis of this scene from a simple record of three boys strolling across a trash-littered parking lot to a dramatic pattern of bold black and gray shapes. Notice the white beverage can and the broken glass texture in the corner of the building shadow. Cover that area and see how their absence alters the visual balance of the composition. Would you like the picture better if the building shadow were solid black?

Figure 9.4a
This photograph was intended to emphasize the rough texture of the stucco wall on which this outdoor mural was painted. Although the texture is visible, the soft light from an overcast sky has reduced the contrast and minimized the effect of surface roughness.

Figure 9.4b
A few minutes later, when the sun appeared, the more direct light described the surface texture much more clearly.

Figure 9.5a
When you find yourself faced with an ordinary unexciting subject, don't just shoot and run. The subject may never make a great picture under any circumstances, but it's very likely that the visual emphasis will vary under different conditions of daylight or weather—or season of the year, if you have the time and patience to wait! This building complex is just a dark mass against the white sky and the pedestrian walkway is unremarkable from this viewpoint. The subject is bland and pointless in this early afternoon summer sunshine.

Figure 9.5b
At sunset the building at right is lighter and well-detailed and the tower at left has virtually disappeared against the white sky background. The slanting pattern of tree shadows adds some textural and spatial interest to the walkway and the wall at right.

For this reason, as you study your subject, you'll probably find it difficult to visualize the general patterns or light and shade that will eventually become part of the compositional structure of your photograph. Those patterns and effects will be obvious enough in the prints, though, and you may be surprised by what the camera has recorded.

Practice will help you learn to handle light effectively. Find a subject that you can return to repeatedly at different times of day , and photograph it under a variety of natural light conditions, figures 9.5a, b, c, d, e. Try to remember your visual impression of each situation and compare it with the print image. When you've learned to recognize and appreciate the quality of light—and take advantage of it—you'll find it much easier to make effective, attractive photographs, figure 9.6.

Figure 9.5c
At dusk the buildings are gray but clearly 3-dimensional and nicely textured. The glass-covered overpass now reflects brightly and the street and building lights are coming on.

Figure 9.5d
At midnight the city lights have—surprisingly—kept the sky quite light, and reflected light is sufficiently strong to reveal considerable detail and texture in the buildings and the grassy foreground. The streetlights are now dominant, and their glare has lightened and emphasized the wall in the right foreground. The blurred figure of the man is recognizable because he walked directly toward the camera for the entire 20-second exposure. Several other people who strolled across the walkway during that time were not recorded.

Figure 9.5e
During a late morning thunderstorm, the gloomy light and wet surfaces provide a still different impression. Notice how clearly the figures are outlined against the glare from the wet walkway, and how obvious the white car is in its gray surroundings. None of these versions can be called a great photograph but each has a distinctive character. Which do you think is the most effective?

Figure 9.6
It's hard to beat the effect of sunlight on ice-covered branches for sheer visual impact, but it's not easy to capture that visual effect in a photograph. In this instance a very wide-angle camera has emphasized the angular divergence of the tree shadows and added to the impression of spatial depth. The glaring reflection from the ice-covered picnic table provides a geometric element that contrasts satisfyingly with the swarming texture of the underbrush, and the unusual lens flare patterns add a dramatic, unearthly note. Under ordinary light conditions this subject would hardly warrant a second glance. Light alone has given this photograph whatever dramatic appeal it may have.

10

Film Exposure

Close Friends.

Photograph by David Alan Jay

The delicate gradation and sharply focused details of this disarmingly simple photograph emphasize the charm of these two young subjects.

There are four things to consider in determining proper film exposure. They are:

1. The sensitivity of the film itself—that is, its *ISO speed.*
2. The brightness (*luminance*) of the subject.
3. The *relative aperture* (*f-number*) or size of the lens opening.
4. The *shutter speed* or exposure interval.

You can think of "proper exposure" as a large weight that must be balanced on a scale with some combination of four smaller weights, each of which must be selected from a different group: film speed; subject luminance; lens aperture; and exposure time, figure 10.1.

In this analogy it's easy to see that if you're faced with a small value of subject luminance (dark subject) and you choose a small value of film speed (slow film), you might choose a relatively large value of aperture (small f-number) and a correspondingly small value of exposure time (or vice versa), or medium values of both. In fact, it's apparent that any combination of small, medium, and large values will work as long their combined "weight" is sufficient to "balance the scale."

In practice, you should set the ISO film speed number into the camera when you load the film. This important first step "places the first weight on the scale," and limits your subsequent choices. The meter measures the subject's luminance (brightness), which "selects the second weight," and restricts your remaining options still further. Your final choices of aperture size and exposure time must now combine to make up the balance. Notice that a change in any one of the values will require some compensating change in one or more of the others.

Although modern black-and-white films have considerable *latitude,* and are therefore quite tolerant of minor exposure errors, well-exposed negatives are easiest to print and generally yield the best image quality. Overexposure will result in *dense* negatives in which even the relatively *thin* shadow tones are much darker than the clear film borders outside the image area, figure 10.2. Underexposed negatives, on the other hand, can be readily identified by their very thin shadow areas in which desirable image detail or texture is only barely visible or, in extreme cases, entirely absent, figure 10.3.

Figure 10.1
Correct film exposure requires an appropriate balance of subject luminance (light), film speed, aperture size, and shutter speed (exposure time).

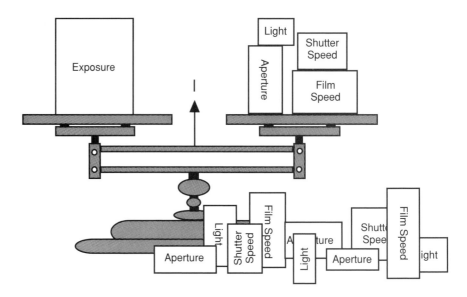

Figure 10.2
This is what an overexposed negative can look like, when seen on a light box. This illustrates severe overexposure that will usually result in some loss of image quality, but sometimes you may be able to make a reasonably satisfactory print from a negative of this sort.

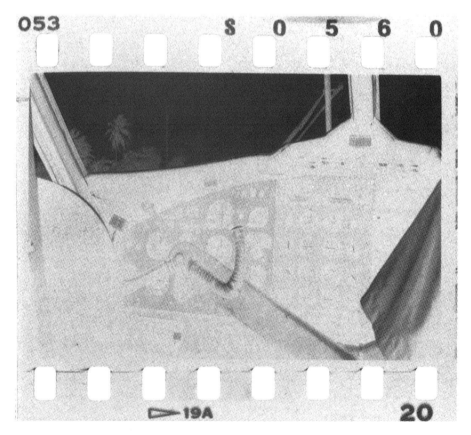

Figure 10.3
This seriously underexposed negative is an almost total loss. There is just a trace of detail in the shadow area but it will print weakly, at best, and the window details will certainly be lost.

Figure 10.4
This print was made from the negative shown in figure 10.2. Print quality is surprisingly good, with excellent shadow detail, but the highlights are slightly grayed and highlight contrast is low.

A moderate degree of overexposure is not likely to be disastrous because all of the negative image details will probably be well-for med. Their greater-than-normal density will require greater-than-normal print exposure but aside from some possible increase in image *graininess* the print quality will probably be quite acceptable, figure 10.4. Shadow detail in prints made from overexposed negatives is generally very good but in extreme cases the negative highlights may begin to *block up* and the print highlights may lose detail and appear chalky.

Underexposure is likely to be more serious because image shadow detail or texture that is lost can't be restored by varying your printing technique. Prints from seriously underexposed negatives will exhibit black, "empty" shadows, the middle tones will appear darker than normal and the highlight areas usually appear harsh and contrasty, figure 10.5.

It's obviously best to expose your film normally but you may not always be sure what "normal" is. In those situations it's a good idea to make at least one exposure that you *think* is "normal," then *bracket* that exposure by deliberately underexposing the next frame by one stop and deliberately overexposing the following frame by one stop.

For example, if you think an exposure of 1/60th second @ f/11 is normal, bracket by exposing the next frame at 1/60th @ f/16, and the following frame at 1/60th @ f/8. Of course, if you prefer to leave the aperture setting alone, you can bracket with the shutter speed, in which case the bracket exposures will be 1/125th @ f/11 and 1/30th @ f/11.

If the situation is so puzzling that you can't decide what the normal exposure should be, use your best guess and bracket by one and two stops for a total of five film frames, figures 10.6 and 10.7a, b, c, d, e. Don't get carried away, though; bracketing is wasteful and not really necessary very often. Think of it as an emergency procedure.

To review:

- The ISO number defines the film's light requirement.
- The meter measures the light to see how much is available.
- The lens aperture setting (f-number) regulates the proportion or intensity of subject light that's allowed to enter the camera.
- The shutter speed setting controls the exposure time.

Figure 10.5
This is a print from the negative shown in figure 10.3. Aside from its dubious value as a record, it is unacceptable. Shadow separation in the negative is so poor that printing for a satisfactory black tone would obscure the print shadow details.

Figure 10.6
When you're unsure of the exposure it's often wise to "bracket" by deliberately underexposing and overexposing a frame or two. This strip of 5 negatives illustrates a 2-stop bracket. From left to right the exposures are: 2 stops under (exposed); 1 stop under; normal; 1 stop over (exposed); and 2 stops over. Compare these negatives with their prints.

Figure 10.7a
The print exposure for the prints in this series (10 seconds) was chosen to produce a good print from the normally exposed negative. Keeping the print exposure constant for all negatives in the series dramatizes the effect of *film exposure* (and therefore *negative density*) on print density or darkness. In other words, this series demonstrates that, for any given print exposure, thin negatives tend to make dark prints and dense negatives print light. The numbers in the print corners indicate the exposure compensation, in stops, that was given to each negative. This print was made from the negative that was underexposed by two stops.

You won't normally have to concern yourself with these four items individually unless you are using a totally manual camera and a separate handheld exposure meter. Even then you probably won't have much control over the subject luminance (unless you resort to artificial lighting of some sort) so there are really only three choices; and one of those (film speed) is eliminated as soon as the camera is loaded and the film speed value has been set into the meter's ISO window.

That leaves only the camera settings themselves. You will usually choose one of them (either aperture or shutter speed) and the meter will tell you what the other should be—assuming that there's enough light on the subject to make a proper exposure possible.

Figure 10.7b
The negative from which this print was made was underexposed by one stop.

Figure 10.7c
This negative was exposed normally and this print is presumably the best one in the series.

Figure 10.7d
This print was made from the negative that was overexposed by one stop.

Figure 10.7e
This print was made from the 2-stop overexposed negative.

CHAPTER 11

Filters

Untitled.

Photograph by Jim Shaffer

Figure 11.1
Filters are available in various colors
and sizes and many are mounted in
threaded rings that can be screwed
directly into the front flange of the
lens mount.

lthough filters are available in several forms, the most common ones are colored glass or plastic disks that can be screwed into the threaded front flange of the camera lens, figure 11.1. In color photography they're used to shift the color of the image—either to correct some inappropriate light condition or to create some special visual or interpretative effect. In black-and-white photography they're used to alter the *gradation* of the image by partially absorbing certain subject colors so that they appear darker than normal in the print image.

For example, a red filter allows red light to enter the camera without much restriction, but absorbs blue-green light strongly. Because of this, red objects are rendered much brighter than they normally appear, and may even approach white in the final black-and-white print. Blue-green objects are rendered very much darker than they appear, and may seem to be nearly black in the print. Other colors are also affected to some degree, but neutral tones—black, grays, and white—will appear quite normal in the final print image, figures 11.2, 3.

Figure 11.2
Without any filtration the film recorded this dark red stop sign as dark gray with bright white letters. The street signs above the stop sign have yellow letters on dark blue background. By rendering the yellow a little darker than it appears and the blue lighter than it appears, the film has reduced the visual contrast and the signs almost disappear into the foliage behind them.

Figure 11.3
A red filter over the lens lightens the red sign to light gray and reduces the contrast of the letters dramatically. The filter also lightens the yellow letters of the street signs and darkens the blue background so the street names are now clearly legible. Compare the values of the other signs in these photographs. Can you guess which areas are colored and which are neutral gray?

Figure 11.4
These Deptford Pinks, photographed without filtration, show up quite clearly against the surrounding grass stems but there is some background interference behind the center blossom.

This ability to lighten or darken colors selectively makes filters very useful in a variety of photographic situations. For example, a landscape photographer might use one to darken the blue of the sky and emphasize white cloud formations. A nature photographer might use a filter to increase the tonal separation between a delicate wildflower and the foliage behind it, figures 11.4, 5, or to emphasize the pattern of a butterfly's wing. A scientific photographer might use a filter to enhance the contrast of a stained microscope specimen; and an

Figure 11.5
A red filter bleaches the pink flower petals to near white and darkens the grass so that the flowers stand out strongly. Although the flowers are not this light, nor the grass this dark in reality, the filtered image is "cleaner" and less confusing.

advertising photographer might use a filter to make the product stand out strongly against its background.

If you can remember two simple principles you'll be able to choose the right filter for just about any situation that requires one. First, a filter will lighten its own color and darken its *complementary color* in the final print; and second, the filter effect is greatest when both the filter color and the subject color are pure and intense.

Figure 11.6
Summer haze had grayed the blue sky when this photograph was made and the unfiltered film recorded it as almost white.

Figure 11.7
A medium yellow filter darkened the blue slightly and has recorded the clouds about as they appeared to the eye.

Thus, the landscape photographer should logically choose a pale yellow filter to add just a hint of tone to the blue sky, or a medium yellow filter to darken it moderately, figures 11.6, 7. For more dramatic effects an orange filter can turn the blue sky medium gray, figure 11.8, and a deep red filter may, under the right conditions, turn the sky almost black, leaving the clouds brilliantly white.

Because filters do their work by absorbing part of the light that would normally enter the camera, they reduce the intensity of the light that reaches the film. To compensate for this light loss you will have to increase the exposure somewhat, and this necessary increase is generally indicated by a number called the *filter factor*, figure 11.9. For example, if a given filter is assigned a factor of 2x it means that you should double the normal exposure when using that filter over the camera lens. You can accomplish this either by opening the lens up one stop, or by doubling the exposure time.

Figure 11.8
An orange filter made the sky look clearer than it really was but the effect is not unreal or overly dramatic.

Film Type	Filter Color			
	Med. Yellow	Yellow-Green	Orange	Red
Ilford HP5 FP4 PanF	*2 / 1.5	3.5 / 4	2 / 1.5	6 / 4
Kodak TMX TMY	1.5 / 2	3 / 3	2 / 1.5	8 / 4
Kodak TMZ	1.5 / 1.2	3 / 3	1.5 / 1.5	6 / 4

Filter Factors for *Daylight / Tungsten

Figure 11.9
Filter factors for several common filters and some popular film types. These factor numbers represent the exposure increase that's required when a filter is used. Notice that the factors for use in daylight and tungsten (ordinary incandescent) light are usually different. That's because daylight is bluish (so it's partially absorbed by red and yellow filters) and tungsten light is relatively yellow-brown (so it tends to pass through red and yellow filters quite easily).

Remember that the factors are multipliers, not stops; that is, a factor of 4x requires a 2-stop increase; 8x equals 3 stops; 16x equals 4 stops, and so on. Estimate the correction needed for other factor numbers as accurately as you can, but absolute precision is not necessary. For example, a factor of 5x represents about 2 1/3 stops, but 2 1/2 is close enough; also 3x equals almost 1 3/5 stops but 1 1/2 will certainly be satisfactory.

When you're doing these calculations, here's one more general principle to keep in mind: a slight degree of underexposure often tends to emphasize the filter effect, while overexposure often reduces it somewhat.

Polarizing filters are neutral gray and have no selective effect on colors, but they have the unique ability to eliminate or reduce surface glare under some conditions. This is possible because the polarizing material in the filter acts like a sort of Venetian blind that figuratively "combs" the light passing through it into parallel sheets. However, if two polarizers are "crossed"— that is, if the "slots" in one are at right angles to the "slots" in the other—light that is polarized by one can't pass through the other, figure 11.10.

Figure 11.10
Two sheets of plastic polarizing material are partially crossed to demonstrate the fact that light that's polarized by one is strongly absorbed by the other. The camera filter's plane of polarization is nearly parallel to that of the upper sheet, but opposes the plane of the lower sheet. Light passes easily through parallel polarizers, but is almost totally blocked when the planes are crossed.

Polarizers are effective in reducing glare because light that glances off of most surfaces at a moderate angle is polarized by reflection. You can investigate this effect by holding a polarizing filter to your eye and rotating it slowly while you observe various objects and surfaces in the light. You'll discover, for example, that (at certain angles) you can eliminate most of the surface glare from water, glass, painted surfaces, and many other materials, but not from bare metals, figures 11.11, 12. You'll also find that the polarizer can darken some areas of the clear blue sky as effectively as a strong red filter can. This effect is related to the sun's position; if you point your finger at the sun, and rotate your hand, your extended thumb will point to the sky arc that's most strongly polarized and can be darkened most completely.

Polarizing filters are particularly useful with color film because they work their magic without altering the hues of the subject. But by removing surface glare they may increase the brilliance and apparent saturation of color, sometimes quite dramatically.

You may have to gain some experience with polarizers to use them effectively. Because you can't see polarized light you can't tell how much of it there is, or how the scene will be affected when photographed through a polarizing filter. Fortunately, as you now know, the filter effect is visible. If your camera is an SLR, attach the filter over your lens and, while studying the viewfinder image, rotate the filter until you like the effect. If you take the picture with the filter in that position the film should record the image just as you saw it.

If your camera is not an SLR, adjusting the polarization is more awkward. Rotate the filter before your eye until you get the desired effect, then without changing its orientation, fix it onto the lens. This will obviously be a problem if the filter is in a simple screw-in mount

Figure 11.11

Figure 11.12

but you can solve the problem by marking the filter ring (or by noting the lettering on the ring itself) to identify the top. Then be sure the mark remains in that position when the filter is installed.

To make this task easier many polarizers are mounted in a ring that can be turned independently of the threads so you can easily adjust the filter to any position without having to leave it loosely mounted. Beware, though; some lenses rotate when they are focused and the filter will rotate with them so that the polarization effect will change. If your lens is one of these, be sure to focus carefully *before* you adjust the filter's position.

Polarizing filters require some exposure increase, just as other filters do, but polarizers don't have any fixed factor. This is because the amount of light they absorb varies. In some cases there may be very little polarized light in the scene, or the filter may be positioned so that the existing polarized light passes through it without attenuation. In these instances the polarizer acts simply as a gray *neutral density filter* and the appropriate factor is about 2x.

On the other extreme, if a large proportion of the subject light is polarized and the filter is positioned to absorb it, the light may be reduced by 2 or more stops.

Because of this uncertainty, it's a good idea to bracket any exposures you make while using a polarizer. Calculate the proper unfiltered exposure, and increase it by 2x (1 stop) to make the first exposure. This exposure is probably the correct one if there is no polarized light to be absorbed, so we'll call it "normal." Then expose

Figure 11.11
The reflection in the window of John's Barber Shop conceals the interior of the shop almost completely.

Figure 11.12
A polarizing filter fitted over the lens, and properly oriented, removes almost all of the reflection and reveals a sign that says the shop is closed.

one or two more frames, doubling the exposure each time for a bracket series that includes "normal," "normal" plus 1 stop, and "normal" plus 2 stops. There is almost never any need to include a less-than-"normal" frame in the series unless you are unsure of the basic, unfiltered exposure.

If your camera is an SLR it may occur to you that you can fix a filter over the lens and let the camera's built-in meter read the filtered light. Then the meter should automatically include the necessary filter factor compensation in calculating the exposure. In many cases this will work well and it can simplify the use of filters considerably. But there are some potential problems: most camera meters are more sensitive to red light than most films are, and will appraise red-filtered light as more intense than it actually is. The meter will therefore recommend less exposure compensation than the filter factor calls for, which will tend to underexpose the film.

Also, some built-in meters are constructed in such a way that they partially polarize the image light. This effect is usually harmless unless you use a polarizer over the lens, in which case some of the light that it passes may be absorbed by the meter itself to cause a false light reading. Check your camera's instruction manual; if it warns of this problem, remove the polarizer while taking your meter readings, then install it and bracket your exposure as described above. If your meter does not affect polarized light (and many do not) it's probably safe to leave the filter in place when you take the readings, and depend on the meter to calculate the correct exposure.

Filters of any kind add two more air-to-glass surfaces to the lens system and will increase flare slightly. This is usually insignificant if the filter surfaces are clean, but if the filter is soiled or dusty it may diffuse the light enough to reduce image contrast noticeably.

Some photographers recommend keeping a clear glass "filter" on the camera lens at all times to protect the lens surface. This is certainly a good idea when you are using your camera in hazardous environments, and may be worthwhile for general use if you're careful to keep the "filter" clean. At worst it may increase flare a little, but at best it may someday save the lens from serious damage.

12
Film Processing: Preparation

Bomb Destruction, Belfast.

Photograph by David Alan Jay

Most of Jay's photographs involve people in informal settings.
In this uncharacteristic photograph he presents an image of
disaster in meticulous detail and beautiful tonality.

E xposing film in the camera is the first step in making a photograph but the exposed film must be *processed* in a series of chemical solutions to produce a useful *negative*. These chemical steps may include most or all of the following:

A *developer* solution that makes the latent image visible.

A *stop bath* that neutralizes the developer and halts development.

A *fixing bath* that removes the unused light-sensitive compounds from the film emulsion.

A *clearing bath* or *washing aid* that helps to remove the absorbed chemicals from the emulsion.

A *washing step*, in running water, to complete the chemical removal.

A *wetting bath* that helps to prevent water spots and promotes even drying.

Handling Precautions

The **developer** solution typically contains several chemical ingredients including one or more *reducing agents* that do the actual work of producing the silver image from the exposed emulsion material. There are several practical reducing agents in common use and most of them are capable of causing allergic reactions in people who are sensitive to them. Fortunately, most people are not affected initially, but after months or years of handling developer solutions some individuals may become sensitized and experience rather serious skin irritation. For this reason it's wise to avoid unnecessary skin contact with all developers even though they may not seem to affect you at all.

In fact, it's prudent to wear protective rubber or plastic gloves while handling *all* photographic chemicals. However, if that's inconvenient or impossible, at least keep your hands out of the developer solutions as much as is practical, and rinse all chemicals off of your hands soon after contact.

The **stop bath** is usually just a very weak solution of acetic acid—about one-third as strong as table vinegar. Although concentrated acetic acid is dangerous, this extremely diluted solution is totally harmless. In fact, if you have had your hands in the developer, rinsing them in the stop bath will neutralize the "soapy" feel and make a following water rinse more effective.

The **fixing bath** is a fairly concentrated mixture of several chemicals but is not likely to harm you in normal use. It can harm film and printing paper, though, and is a potentially serious darkroom contaminant. Be sure to wash it off of your hands before handling *anything*, including light switches, faucet handles, utensils, or—especially—sensitized materials.

The **clearing bath** or **washing aid** is another relatively harmless solution that requires no special handling. It is not absolutely essential to the process but is recommended because it can reduce the final wash time appreciably.

The **wash** step is necessary to remove the processing chemicals from the film to help protect the image from eventual fading or discoloration.

The **wetting bath** is a final water rinse to which a small quantity of some wetting agent has been added. It's purpose is to reduce the surface tension so that the water will "sheet" off of the film surface instead of forming droplets which can cause permanent *water spots* on the negatives. The wetting bath is harmless but because it works like a detergent, prolonged exposure can remove some of the oil from your skin and make your hands feel dry.

Preparing the Chemical Solutions

Film developers are sold either as packets of dry chemicals to be mixed with water, or as concentrated solutions to be diluted for use. If you choose a powdered developer, such as Kodak's D-76 or Ilford's ID-11 Plus, I suggest that you prepare the solution several hours before you plan to use it.

There are two reasons for this: first, the mixing instructions usually specify fairly hot water so that the chemicals will dissolve easily, and the solution will require some time to cool down to usable temperature. More importantly, though, the dry chemical powders may not dissolve immediately and completely even though the solution appears to be clear. Although you can probably cool the solution and use it almost immediately with satisfactory results, it's a good idea to wait until it cools naturally. By that time the solution should be complete and stable.

Liquid concentrates can be diluted and used immediately but be sure to read and follow the instructions carefully because they may be a little confusing. This is because some concentrates, such as Kodak's HC-110 and Ilford's ILFOTEC HC, are frequently diluted, for convenience, to form intermediate stock solutions that are still highly potent and must be further diluted.

These two developers in particular are supplied as highly concentrated syrups that must be diluted with from about 15 to 79 (or more) parts of water for use. Because it's difficult to measure very small volumes of the syrupy liquid with any sort of accuracy, both manufacturers recommend diluting the syrup with 3 parts of water to make an intermediate *stock solution* that is further diluted to prepare the *working solution* that you will actually use. I recommend this, too; just be sure to label the stock solution bottle clearly, and include on the label the mixing instructions for the working solutions that you prefer.

Most other liquid developers come already prepared as stock solutions. Typically they are diluted with from about 3 to 9 parts of water to prepare working solutions. There's not much chance for confusion here if you follow the instructions. Just be sure you don't use the concentrate as a working solution, or dilute the working solution twice!

Although it's possible to save some film developers after use and *replenish* them for reuse, I don't recommend it. In general I think you'll find it easier and more satisfactory to use your developer as a *one-shot;*

that is, mix the working solution fresh each time, use it, and discard it. In fact, the working solutions of most developers deteriorate much more rapidly than their stock solutions, and some may not work reliably if they're more than a few hours old, whether they've been used previously or not.

If you plan to keep a developer stock solution for more than just a few days it's a good idea to store it in full brown bottles in a fairly cool, dark place, to minimize its exposure to air and light. For example, if you have mixed a gallon of D-76 or ID-11 I suggest that you store it in 4 1-quart bottles rather than in a single gallon container. Also, because developers are particularly susceptible to oxidation, it's best to keep their stock solutions in brown glass bottles. Plastic bottles are fine for most other chemical solutions but because they "breathe" they're not as appropriate for developer storage.

Incidentally, although D-76, in particular, is a fine developer with many desirable characteristics, it does not keep very well and should be used up within a month or so for best results, even if stored under good conditions.

The **stop bath** stock solution is usually supplied as a 28% solution of acetic acid, but a much more dangerous form of 99% strength, called "glacial acetic acid," is also available. Be sure you are using the 28% solution. The plain acid solution is clear and colorless; if it appears strongly yellow it contains a pH-sensitive *indicator dye* that will change to purple when the acid is neutralized in use.

Acetic acid has a powerful, penetrating odor and should be handled only in a well-ventilated area. Prepare the working solution for film processing by adding about 1 part of the 28% acid concentrate to from 20 to 27 parts of water. This will produce a bath whose acid strength is from about 1.33% to 1%. For example:

To make (working solution)	Add 28% stock	To water
8 fluid ounces	1/3 fl. oz.	7 2/3 fl. oz.
12 fl. oz.	1/2 fl. oz.	11 1/2 fl. oz.
32 fl. oz.	1 1/4 fl. oz.	30 3/4 fl. oz.

Although the prepared stop bath solution can be reused for several rolls of film before it's likely to become neutralized, it's not worth saving. I suggest that you mix it fresh for each developing session, then discard it.

The **fixing bath** may also be supplied as either a powder or as a liquid concentrate although the liquid concentrates are much more common now. The two forms are fundamentally different. The powder form makes a relatively mild solution that's composed mainly of sodium thiosulfate; the liquid form uses ammonium thiosulfate and is commonly referred to as "rapid fix" because of its greater strength. Both types are often called simply *hypo*—a term that was erroneously applied to the sodium salt about 150 years ago and has since become a permanent part of photographic lore.

Rapid fixing bath concentrates are typically diluted with about 3 or 4 parts of water for use with films, and they are usually supplied with a separate bottle of hardener solution that may be added to the fixing bath to toughen the film's gelatin emulsion when that's considered desirable. Hardeners are not as important now as they used to be because modern film emulsions are tough enough to withstand ordinary handling just as they come from the factory. It's probably a good idea to include the hardener, though, especially if you must process the film at fairly high temperature.

Follow the mixing instructions carefully when preparing either type of fixer. If mixed carelessly—that is, with water that's too hot, or with inadequate stirring—both types are likely to produce milky solutions that result from partial decomposition of the thiosulfate. This problem is particularly likely to occur if you add the hardener to the undiluted fixer, or to a solution that has not been properly blended by stirring. In some cases the milky precipitate will redissolve after the solution has stood for a while but if it does not the fixer should be discarded. Although a milky bath will probably fix the film there is some danger that it will also contribute to eventual fading or discoloration of the negative image.

The fixing bath can be reused for several rolls of film and it's wasteful to throw it away after a single use. Save it in a well-marked bottle and keep track of the number of rolls of film that it has treated. As a general rule you should be able to fix about 8 to 12 rolls of 35mm film in 16 fluid ounces of fixer (about 60 to 100 rolls per gallon) before it becomes dangerously weak or contaminated. However, KODAK's popular T-MAX ("tabular grain") films—and presumably films of similar type by other manufacturers—will exhaust the fixer relatively rapidly. To be safe you should probably monitor the fixer's condition periodically by using any of the " hypo test" solutions that are available from any well-stocked photography store.

Again, remember that the fixing bath is destructive to undeveloped films and papers. Get into the habit of washing everything it touches and always wash your hands after using it. If your darkroom shows signs of dried hypo scums on its various surfaces you can almost certainly expect to find streaks and spots on your negatives and prints, sooner or later.

The **(hypo) clearing bath** is optional but generally recommended. It can be prepared from any of several available powders or liquid concentrates. The liquid concentrates are most convenient to use but mixing instructions vary so follow the manufacturer's instructions. Unless those instructions specifically recommend saving and reusing the bath I suggest that you mix it fresh for each developing session, then discard it.

The **wetting bath** should ideally be prepared with distilled water to avoid the possible formation of mineral deposit scums on your negatives. There are several common brands of wetting agents that are designed for photographic use and they are essentially similar. In general, following the manufacturers' recommendations for preparing the working bath will result in a stronger solution than is necessary and may actually contribute to greasy deposits on the backs of the negatives.

I suggest increasing the dilution experimentally until it's too weak to prevent water droplets from forming on the back of the film when it's hung up to dry. Then increase the amount of concentrate again until the solution "wets" the film smoothly without forming droplets. In other words, make this bath just strong enough to do the job, but no stronger.

Use the wetting bath for all the films you process in one session, then discard it.

Equipment

Rollfilms of all sizes are processed most easily, manually, in special *tanks*. There are two types. The popular stainless steel models are most expensive and most difficult for beginners to use, but they're compact and durable, and preferred by many experienced photographers. Plastic tanks—the other popular variety—are probably most appropriate for beginners because they're relatively inexpensive and easy to load. Either type is capable of good results if handled properly.

Whether you prefer plastic or stainless steel, I suggest that you buy a tank that will accommodate two film *reels* rather than just a single one, even if you have no intention of developing two rolls of film at a time. Get the second reel, too, and use it as a "spacer" for better and more consistent results when you're processing only a single roll.

Because the rate of film development is related more or less directly to the temperature of the developer, it's important to control the temperature quite closely. I recommend that you buy a good photographic thermometer and handle it carefully to preserve its accuracy. The "dial" types with the stainless steel stem are moderately expensive but they're accurate, responsive, durable, and reliable. I recommend them.

Cleanliness

Cleanliness is essential if you hope to do good work in your darkroom. I suggest that you add to your equipment list a full-size apron, some rubber or plastic gloves, one or two old towels, and a large plastic sponge. Wear the apron for all darkroom procedures and carry a towel with you, perhaps tucked in your belt or pinned to the apron, as you work. Wear the protective gloves whenever you're mixing chemicals and while you're using the developer solutions. Use the sponge to clean up spilled liquids, then rinse it clean.

Whether you're wearing the gloves or not, get into the habit of washing your hands after every chemical contact, and wipe them dry on the towel before proceeding. NEVER wipe chemical liquids off your hands onto the towel! ALWAYS wash first! Then wash your darkroom towels frequently to keep them clean and free from chemical contamination. These simple precautions can help to improve the quality of your work and may save you considerable frustration.

13

Developing Film

Untitled.

Photograph by Jean–Claude Lejeune

Film that has been properly exposed in the camera has been photochemically altered to produce a *latent* image but chemical development is required to make the image visible. The film developer solution accomplishes this by reducing the exposed silver salts in the film emulsion to form fine particles of metallic silver. These minute particles, massed densely in some areas and thinly in others, produce the film image. Because the silver image is densest in areas of the film that received the greatest exposure to light, the image tones appear reversed, so we call the image a *negative*.

Although film exposure can be almost instantaneous, development takes time because the chemical action proceeds quite slowly. During development the density of the various image areas increases more or less in proportion to the amount of exposure each received so the image contrast—the density difference between highlight and shadow areas—increases progressively. It's important to let development proceed long enough to form an image of sufficient contrast, but the process must be halted before the image becomes *too* contrasty to print easily.

Development is also affected by several other factors, each of which must be considered and controlled:

- The type of developer is one factor; some developers are stronger than others and build up image density more rapidly. When one of these vigorous solutions is used, development time should be reduced appropriately.

- Developer dilution slows the rate of development, but not all developers are affected to the same degree. Again, the effects of developer dilution must be compensated in some way, usually by increasing the development time.

- Temperature is a significant factor; warm developer solutions work more vigorously than cool solutions, so the time of development must be adjusted to compensate for variations in temperature.

- Finally, agitation—stirring or sloshing the developer during development—increases the rate of development.

Although any of these factors *can* be varied to control development, not all are equally useful or effective. Increasing the temperature, for example, may soften the film emulsion dangerously, and varying the agitation can result in uneven development that can show up in your prints as mottled tones or streaks. As a general rule it's best to standardize developer type, dilution, temperature, and agitation, and vary only development *time* as necessary to control negative contrast.

Determining Development Time

Your printing conditions really dictate film developing time. Because the printing paper is fairly inflexible it needs negatives of rather specific contrast in order to produce good, full-scale print images. "Normal" film development time is whatever time is required to produce a negative of this desired contrast from films that have been exposed to "normal" subjects.

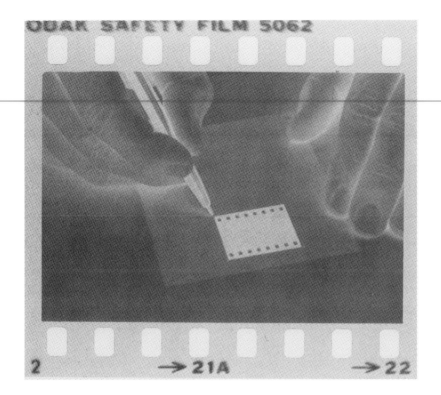

Figure 13.1
You can tell that this very flat (low contrast) negative has been underdeveloped rather than underexposed, because even the thinnest areas (corresponding to the darkest portions of the subject) display usable density. An underexposed negative might also appear to be flat but its shadow areas will appear very thin and lacking in detail.

As you can see, this is a pretty loose definition because it depends on the type of printing paper you like to use (not all require negatives of the same contrast). It also depends on the type of enlarger you print with: *condenser enlargers* tend to produce fairly high contrast; *diffusion enlargers* generally produce less contrast.

The film manufacturers publish development recommendations for their films and developers but these recommendations shouldn't be taken too literally. They're generally based on the assumption that you'll print with a diffusion enlarger and that your paper needs negatives of average contrast. If these assumptions don't apply in your situation, using the manufacturer's recommended development times may produce negatives that you'll find difficult to print.

The published times are a starting point, however. You can test them by exposing a short roll of film to a variety of subjects under ordinary daylight conditions (hazy sunlight generally provides "normal" contrast) and developing for the recommended time. Be sure to control both developer temperature and agitation as recommended. Then inspect the negatives on a light box.

In general, *film exposure* is responsible for variations in overall image *density* or darkness—that is, the entire area of an overexposed negative will be quite dark, and a seriously underexposed negative will have "thin" areas where almost no trace of image tone is evident, see figures 10.2,3.

Development variations affect overall density too, to some extent, but image *contrast* is altered most obviously. If your test negatives appear relatively "weak" or gray, without much difference between shadow and highlight densities, they've probably been underdeveloped, figure 13.1. On the other hand, if they are obviously contrasty, with dense highlight areas and relatively thin, transparent shadows, they've probably been overdeveloped, figure 13.2.

Figure 13.2
The excessive contrast of this negative indicates that it has been given too much development for this very long range (high contrast) subject.

Figure 13.3
This print, made on normal paper from the negative in figure 13.1, is well-detailed in both shadow and highlight areas, but lacks the accent tones of black and white. You can conclude from this that either the film development was insufficient for this short range (low contrast) subject, or the printing conditions (paper grade and enlarger type) don't provide enough contrast for this negative. In this case the film development was inadequate and a paper of higher contrast grade will be required to print this negative satisfactorily.

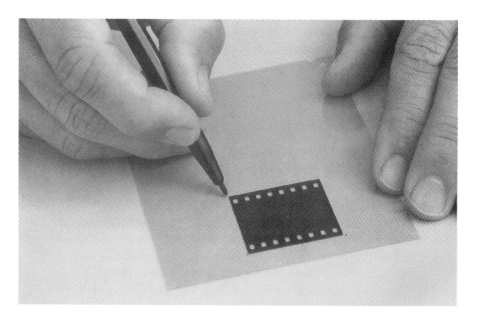

Then try printing the negatives on your chosen paper. If they print easily and produce full-scale prints with good detail in both shadow and light areas, you can consider the film development to have been "normal" for your purposes. If the prints are gray with no real black or white accents, the film was probably underdeveloped, figure 13.3; and if the prints are harshly contrasty without much visible detail in either deep shadow or highlight areas, you've probably overdeveloped the film—at least for use with that paper, figure 13.4.

Figure 13.4
This print, made from the negative in figure 13.2, shows the black, opaque shadow areas and bleached highlights that indicate excessive image contrast. In this case the film was given too much development for this very long range subject, but this same appearance could result from using a high contrast paper to print a normal negative. A soft (low contrast) paper will be required to make a better print from this contrasty negative.

Film exposed to "normal" subjects and developed "normally" will produce "normal" negatives—but, unfortunately, not all subjects are normal. Ideally you should vary the film development to compensate for variations in subject contrast, but that's not usually practical. When you have photographed subjects of different contrasts on a single roll of film, as is usually the case, the best you can do is to develop the roll for your normal time, accepting the fact that only some of the negatives will be normal. This isn't usually as serious as it sounds because printing papers are available in a wide range of *contrast grades* to accommodate negatives that are too contrasty or too flat to print normally.

Occasionally, though, you may be able to expose an entire roll of film to subjects of similar contrast, or you may be so interested in a few unusual subjects that you're willing to adjust development to favor them. In these cases you can deliberately "over-" or "underdevelop" the roll to make certain negatives easier to print, perhaps at the risk of sacrificing a few of the less valuable exposures.

If you want to experiment with this method, learn to recognize the difference among subjects of "normal range," "long range," (high contrast) and "short range" (low contrast). In general, subjects which include both intense light and deep shadow, such as scenes in brilliant sunshine, or rock concerts where the performers are spotlighted, can be called "long range," and should be given reduced development to keep image contrast under control. "Short range" subjects might include outdoor scenes under heavy overcast or in mist or fog, and subjects that are completely in shade even on a bright day.

As a rule of thumb, if you want to vary development to adjust image contrast, multiply your normal development time by about 1.4 for short range subjects and by about 0.7 for long range subjects. You can often improve the quality of long range subjects somewhat by overexposing a half-stop or so to compensate for the reduced film development time. A similar degree of underexposure is often appropriate when development time can be extended.

Figure 13.5
This film was rated at 4 times its normal film speed and push-processed in an attempt to compensate for the resulting underexposure of 2 stops. The resulting negative has not recorded detail in the darker areas of the subject and the highlight areas are excessively dense. In other words, the extended development has made the negative extremely contrasty. Moral: you cannot change the speed of a film by simply changing the ISO number that you set into your meter.

Figure 13.6
In printing the "pushed" negative, a soft paper was required to keep the excessive contrast under control and that has further reduced the already inadequate tonal separation in the shadow areas. Although some film/developers handle push-processing better than others do, you'll get better image quality by exposing and developing normally whenever possible.

"Push" Processing

There's a popular misconception that film speed can be increased substantially by *pushing* (significantly extending) development. There is a germ of truth in this but in most instances the useful range is not great and there's a penalty to be paid. The fact is that although film development does influence effective film speed a little, it affects image contrast much more obviously, figure 13.5. Even when the subject range is short, and some development increase is appropriate, *excessive* development is likely to produce harsh image gradation, a noticeable increase in grain size and, in extreme cases, may result in some loss of image sharpness.

In other words, "pushing" film is really just overdeveloping it. "Pushing" can't compensate adequately for insufficient exposure; and whether it's worthwhile or not really depends on how much image quality you're willing to sacrifice, figure 13.6.

Figure 13.7a

The rate and extent of development is controlled most obviously by the development time and the temperature of the developer solution. The recommended developing temperature is generally 68° F, but most developers will function satisfactorily if used in the range between 65° and 75° F. Within that range the actual temperature is less important than consistency; pick a temperature that you can repeat conveniently, and standardize it. For critical control of negative contrast you should maintain the developer at that standard temperature (within 1 degree Fahrenheit) during the development period. The stop bath and fixing bath temperatures are less critical but it's a good idea to keep them within 2 or 3 degrees of the developer temperature— whatever it is. Adjust the solutions' temperatures, if necessary, by setting their bottles in a tray of warm or cold water, as required. While you're waiting for the temperatures to stabilize, you can load your exposed film into the developing tank if you have not already done so.

Figure 13.7b

If you were wearing gloves while preparing the chemicals, take them off. Be sure your hands, the developing tank, film reels, and tank cover are clean and dry. Place the tank parts close at hand so that you can locate them in the dark. Similarly, position a small pair of scissors, your exposed film cartridge, and the tool you'll use to open it—an ordinary bottle or beverage can opener is suitable. Now turn out *all* the lights; do *not* leave a safelight on while handling unprotected film. Find the film cartridge and the opener and pry off the flat end of the cartridge.

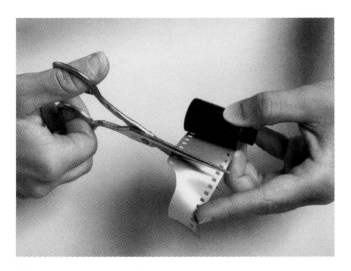

Figure 13.7c

Remove the film spool from the cartridge. Be careful not to let the film spring loose and unwind. You can handle the outside of the film roll safely if your hands are dry. Find the scissors then stretch out the tapered film tongue and cut it off, leaving a square end on the remaining film strip. Alternatively, some photographers prefer not to open the film cartridge at all and, after cutting off the film tongue, simply load the film directly from the cartridge into the tank reel. That method saves time and effort and works well, but pulls the film through the cartridge light trap again, which slightly increases the risk of scratching the film.

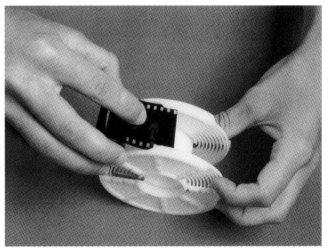

Figure 13.7d

Locate the film reel and find the opening in its perimeter that marks the beginning of the spiral track. This may take some practice because the reel flanges can be easily rotated out of alignment. Line them up, and determine which way the spiral track is headed, by feel; then insert the square-cut end of the film strip into the spiral track opening and feed the film gently into the track, pushing it along until it begins to bind a little. If the reel is dry and the film has not been kinked in handling, you should be able to load 10 or 15 inches of it this way.

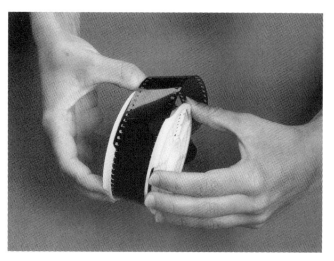

Figure 13.7e
As soon as you feel some resistance, stop trying to simply push the film along and shift your grip to the reel flanges, as shown. Now by simply rotating the flanges back and forth, exerting light finger pressure on the film edge during the advancing stroke, you should be able to "walk" the rest of the film strip onto the reel. This will be easy enough after you've done it a few times, especially if you've practiced previously in the light.

Figure 13.7f
When you reach the end of the film strip, cut off the attached film spool and walk the film a little further onto the reel to be sure the end is safely loaded.

Figure 13.7g
Place the loaded reel on the tank center post. Tank designs differ somewhat but there's probably a right way to do this. If it doesn't slip onto the post easily don't force it. You may have the reel upside down; try it the other way. If you have only a single roll to process be sure to push it all the way to the bottom of the post. It isn't necessary to place an empty reel on top of it in most tanks, but in some types (the popular stainless steel models which have no center post, for example) a single reel is free to flop up and down in the tank during agitation. In that case using the extra reel is advisable. When the reel is correctly positioned on the center post, put the assembly into the tank and put the cover on tightly. The tank is now light-tight and you can work from here on in room light.

Figure 13.7h
If the processing solutions have reached 68° F, or your preferred standard temperature, you're ready to begin. Put on your protective gloves. Determine the proper development time (see figure 13.8), set an interval timer or note the time on a clock or watch, and pour the developer into the tank as quickly as you can without spilling it. If you're processing a single roll fill the tank only far enough to cover the loaded film reel comfortably (it's more difficult to provide good agitation when the tank is full).

Figure 13.7i
As soon as the developer is in the tank put on the cap to prevent the liquids from spilling out and alternately invert the tank and bump it briskly several times against your hand, the sink, or table surface to dislodge any air bells that may have formed on the film surface. Continue this vigorous agitation for 10 or 15 seconds, then put the tank down and let it rest quietly. After about 25 seconds of rest, agitate the tank again by inverting it briskly two or three times in about 5 seconds, then let it rest again. Continue this agitation procedure—2 or 3 vigorous inversions within a 5-second period every 30 seconds—until the time is almost up.

Figure 13.7j
About 15 seconds before the end of the development time, dump the developer down the sink drain or into a waste container. . . .

Figure 13.7k
. . . and immediately pour in the stop bath.

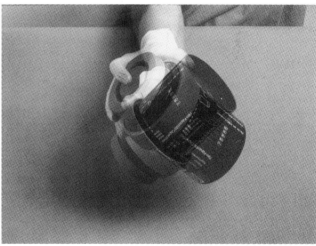

Figure 13.7l
Agitate leisurely for about 30 seconds.

Figure 13.7m
Dump out the stop bath . . . .

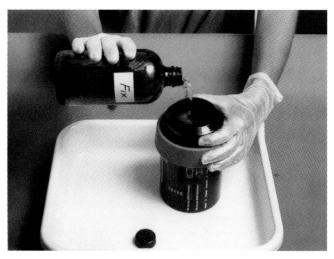

Figure 13.7n
. . . and pour in the fixing bath. Note the time for reference.

Figure 13.7o
Agitate leisurely for about 30 seconds, then let the tank rest for another 30 seconds before removing the cover. Lift the reel out of the fixer and check the film briefly; if there is any sign of milkiness replace the film in the fixer and check it again in 30 seconds. When the film is "clear"—that is, when the milky appearance is gone—note the elapsed time period; the film should remain in the fixing bath, with frequent agitation, for another period of the same length. For example, if it took 2 minutes for the film to clear, it should remain in the fixer for at least 2 more minutes, for a total of 4 minutes. If the clearing time was 3 1/2 minutes, the total should be at least 7 minutes. Consider these times to be minimums; some films, notably KODAK's T-MAX films, fix relatively slowly and require extended fixing to remove a strong magenta dye that is one of the emulsion's ingredients. If you remove a T-MAX film from the fixer before that magenta dye has begun to fade and take on a yellowish or brownish tint, you'll find it very difficult to wash the dye out later. Also, the T-MAX films exhaust fixer more rapidly than some other films do, so check the condition of the film fixer fairly frequently. Remember, when fixing the T-MAX films, more is better than less; let the dye color be your guide.

Figure 13.7p
When the film has been properly fixed, pour the used fixer back into its storage jug. It's a good idea to keep track of the number of film rolls it has been used for. You should be able to fix at least 10—and perhaps as many as 25—rolls of film per quart of film-strength rapid fix before it's exhausted; but it's a good idea to monitor its condition frequently with one of the commercial hypo test solutions. Discard the fixer when it begins to fail the test.

Figure 13.7q
Although the hypo clearing bath is not absolutely necessary, it does aid in the removal of the fixing chemicals, and increases the efficiency of the wash. There are several clearing baths, or washing aids, on the market. Use the one of your choice and follow its instructions for use.

Figure 13.7r
Discard the clearing bath. ...

Figure 13.7s
...and wash the film in running water for the time recommended by the manufacturer of the clearing bath you've used. If you have not used a clearing bath, wash the film for at least 20 minutes. In either case, agitate the film occasionally by lifting the reel completely out of the water, and empty the tank completely several times during the wash period to dislodge a film of air bubbles that may have formed on the film surfaces, and to keep the water fresh.

Figure 13.7t
Prepare the wetting bath with distilled water if it's available and pour it into a small tray. Remove the thoroughly-washed film from the film reel and attach a film clip to each end of the roll. Then "see-saw" it briskly through the wetting bath several times, as illustrated. You can use the wetting bath in the film tank instead of a tray if you prefer, but the tray is a little more convenient.

Figure 13.7u
Finally, stretch the film strip out and hold it at an angle to allow the wetting bath to flow to one edge of the strip and drip off the bottom corner. This will help to float any dirt or lint particles out of the image area and onto the film edge where they're harmless.

Figure 13.7v
Hang the drained film in a drying cabinet or other dust-free environment.

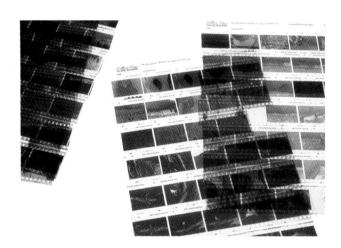

Figure 13.7w
Handle the dry film strip by its edges or wear clean white cotton gloves to avoid marking the negatives with greasy fingerprints. Cut the negatives into strips of 5 and store them in special plastic storage pages that are punched to fit standard notebooks. Alternatively, cut strips of 6 negatives and store them in individual glassine or (preferably) archival plastic envelopes.

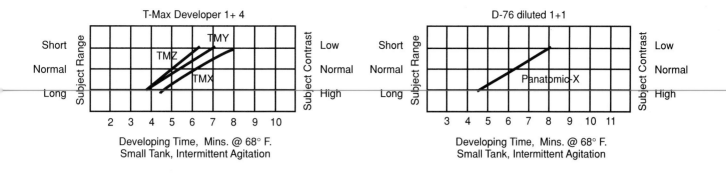

T-Max Developer 1+ 4

Developing Time, Mins. @ 68° F.
Small Tank, Intermittent Agitation

D-76 diluted 1+1

Developing Time, Mins. @ 68° F.
Small Tank, Intermittent Agitation

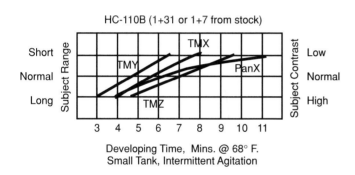

D-76 Straight

Developing Time, Mins. @ 68° F.
Small Tank, Intermittent Agitation

Rodinal 1+ 50

Developing Time, Mins. @ 68° F.
Small Tank, Intermittent Agitation

HC-110B (1+31 or 1+7 from stock)

Developing Time, Mins. @ 68° F.
Small Tank, Intermittent Agitation

Figure 13.8
Consult these charts to find suggested developing times for some popular films and developers. These recommendations assume that you will print on a normal grade #2 paper using a condenser enlarger. However, because papers vary and all enlargers are not alike, you'll probably have to adjust these times for optimum results. When you've arrived at developing times that work well for you, you may want to enter the appropriate data in the chart (figure 13.9) for quick reference.

Figure 13.9

Chart of Personal Developing Times

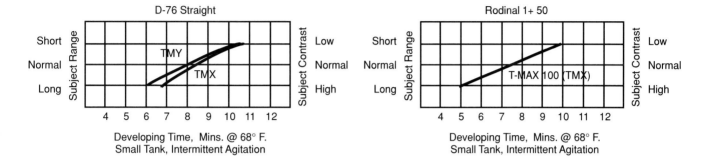

Film Type	Developer	Dilution	Temp.	Time

14
CHAPTER

Printing

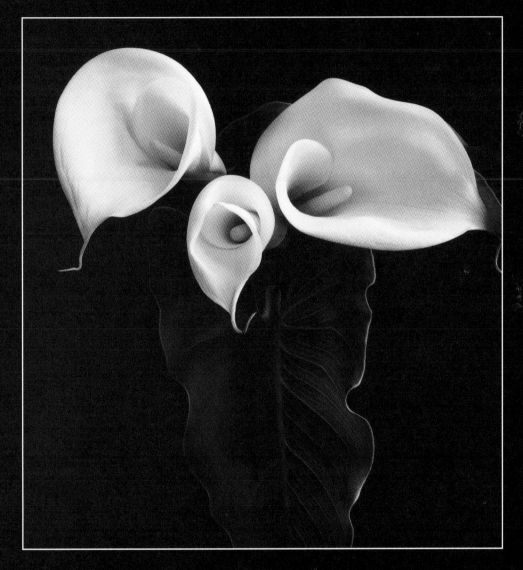

Callas.

Photograph by Kathleen Barrows

In this elegantly simple composition, Barrows again displays her sensitivity
to the quality of light and its effect on form and texture.

You'll probably use an enlarger to make most of your prints so that you can adjust the image size and composition conveniently. There are three enlarger types. You'll be able to make fine-quality prints with any of them, but each has certain advantages.

Condenser enlargers (figure 14.1a) provide very bright light for short printing times; and when the condensers are properly adjusted to match the focal length of the projection lens the image illumination is very uniform. The concentrated illumination tends to provide brilliant image contrast but also emphasizes the effects of minor scratches and dust on the negative as they're reproduced in the print.

Diffusion enlargers (figure 14.1b) provide a "softer" light that tends to subdue negative surface defects and minimize their effects in the print image but printing times may be a little longer and because (by comparison with condensers) diffusion systems reduce image contrast somewhat, they require negatives of higher contrast. Most diffusion enlargers provide uniform illumination at the image plane but some "cold cathode" types may illuminate the print area less evenly.

Color enlargers (figure 14.1c) are generally diffusion enlargers whose design includes a set of three separately-adjustable color filters. These filters can be moved into the light path by external calibrated controls, and the light integrating chamber blends the light mixture

Figure 14.1

a. In a condenser enlarger, the condensers concentrate the light from a tungsten lamp and direct it through the negative into the projection lens. This design provides intense illumination that allows short printing times, and image contrast is typically high.

b. Diffusion systems illuminate the negative with a broad, unfocused light that is less intense, but quite efficient. Image contrast is relatively low.

c. Color heads combine the advantages of a brilliant tungsten light source with the uniform illumination chacteristics of the diffusion systems. A well-designed color head is efficient and convenient for both black-and-white and color printing.

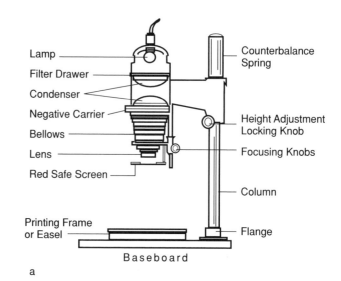

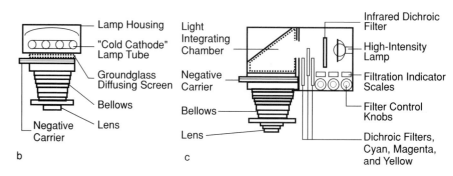

into a uniform tint before it reaches the negative. All three filters (yellow, magenta and cyan) are useful in color printing but the yellow and magenta filters are also very useful for controlling the contrast of variable- or selective-contrast black-and-white printing papers. The third color, cyan, is not necessary for black-and-white work.

If you want to edit your negatives before beginning to enlarge them you may want to *proof* them by *contact printing* them in a *printing frame* or *proofing frame* (figure 14.2). When you've selected a negative to enlarge, it will go in the enlarger's *negative carrier* and the printing paper can be held flat and in position in an *enlarging easel* (figure 14.3) You'll find focusing the projected image easy if you use a *grain focuser.* One type displays a tiny portion of the image on a fine groundglass screen and the other popular type lets you inspect the "aerial image" as it floats in space. Both types provide considerable magnification so that it's relatively easy to focus on the image grain pattern—insuring that the image itself will then be sharply focused.

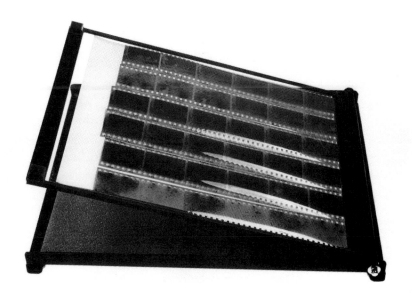

Figure 14.2
Proofing frame

Figure 14.3
Easel

Figure 14.4
Tongs and paddle

Prints are usually developed in trays and handled with *print tongs* to minimize hand contact with the processing chemicals (figure 14.4). If you prefer to handle prints with your fingers it's a good idea to wear protective plastic or latex gloves to protect your hands from chemical contact.

Printing Materials

Printing papers, like films, must be exposed and developed to produce a useful image. The sequence of chemical steps is quite similar but films require relatively mild developers that work slowly and progressively—both to permit control of image contrast and to keep the image grain to a minimum. Papers have no visible grain structure and don't depend on progressive development for contrast control, so paper developers are very much more vigorous and faster working than those we use for films.

The same stop and fixing baths *can* be used for films and papers, but because the print image can be partially bleached by prolonged immersion in strong fixer, we normally make the paper fixing bath only half as strong as film fixer.

It's also important to monitor the condition of the paper fixer by testing it frequently with one of the commercial hypo test solutions. Although fixer solutions will continue to work reasonably well until they're nearly exhausted, prints treated in these old, well-used baths are difficult to wash well, and their images may gradually fade or discolor with age.

Treatment in a hypo clearing bath is optional but recommended for *fiber-base* papers, but *resin-coated* papers should be placed directly into the wash bath after fixing. At this stage some photographers like to *tone* their prints in special chemical solutions but this is rarely done with films. On the other hand, the wetting bath that completes the film processing sequence is almost never used for papers.

The recommendations for the storage and handling of film chemicals (described in a previous chapter) apply equally to paper chemicals. Also, it's important to remember that papers are much more susceptible to chemical stains than films are, so do your best to keep your darkroom utensils and surfaces—and your hands—clean and free from chemical contamination while working with prints.

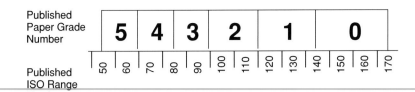

Published Paper Grade Number	5	4	3	2	1	0

| Published ISO Range Number | 50 | 60 | 70 | 80 | 90 | 100 | 110 | 120 | 130 | 140 | 150 | 160 | 170 |

Figure 14.5
There is no official relationship between the conventional paper grade numbers and the ISO Range numbers but this shows their practical equivalence.

Paper Characteristics

Printing papers are available in a wide variety of types, sizes, surface textures, weights, and tints. All are thinly coated—just as films are— with an *emulsion* of light-sensitive silver compounds suspended in gelatin. Papers are much less sensitive than films and, unlike most films which are sensitive to light of all colors, most papers are not sensitive to red or orange light. This fact allows us to handle papers in the dim yellow-brown illumination of a *safelight*. However, even this light is not truly "safe." If it is too bright or if paper is exposed to it for more than just a few minutes it can *fog* the paper and cause noticeable graying of the print image highlights.

Papers differ from films in other respects, too. For example, because films develop slowly and progressively, we can control the contrast of a film image by halting development when the desired image tonality has been attained. This is not feasible with papers because they must be developed "to completion" in order to produce a full black image tone. Extending development much beyond that point doesn't improve the image usefully and simply increases the likelihood of chemical or safelight fog.

Because print contrast isn't ordinarily influenced very much by development variations the manufacturers have supplied us with both fixed-contrast *graded papers* and *variable-contrast papers*. The contrast characteristic of graded papers is indicated by numbers from 0 to 5. The lower numbers (0 and 1) identify papers that will produce low contrast; grade 2 papers are considered to provide normal contrast; and the higher numbers (3, 4, and 5) produce increasingly higher contrast. Some manufacturers also list the relatively recent *ISO Range* numbers as an indication of paper contrast, figure 14.5.

Variable-contrast (VC), also sometimes called "selective-contrast" (SC) papers are not graded themselves but are intended to be exposed through special grade-numbered *printing filters*, figures 14.6a, b, c, d, e, f, g. Typically, exposing these papers to green light produces low contrast and exposure to blue light produces high contrast. We accomplish this in practice by using yellowish filters (which absorb blue but transmit green) for low contrast results, and magenta filters (which absorb green but transmit blue) to produce high contrast images.

Variable-contrast papers are very convenient and economical to use because they eliminate the need to stock separate quantities of paper in the various grades. Also, when used with color enlargers (whose built-in, continuously-variable color filters include yellow and magenta) the available range of contrasts is no longer restricted to specific grades. You can adjust the enlarger's filter dials to provide any degree of contrast you need, figure 1.6.

Figure 14.6a
This series of prints demonstrates the range of contrast control that's provided by a popular variable-contrast paper and its matching set of printing filters. Because the filters absorb part of the printing light these print exposure times had to be adjusted individually in order to maintain a more or less uniform mid-tone density. When a variable-contrast paper is used without any filter it typically produces about the same degree of image contrast that's provided by the #2 (normal) printing filter. This first print was made without any filtration; the exposure time was 8 seconds.

Figure 14.6b
The #0 print filter required a 36-second exposure to produce this print.

Figure 14.6c
This print was exposed for 27 seconds through the #1 filter.

Figure 14.6d
This "normal" print, exposed for 22 seconds through the #2 filter, matches the unfiltered print quite closely.

Figure 14.6e
The #3 filter and a 15-second exposure produced this print.

Figure 14.6f
This print needed a 20-second exposure through the #4 filter.

Figure 14.6g
This harshly contrasty print was made by exposing for 25 seconds, using the #5 printing filter.

The traditional fiber-base papers are generally preferred by art photographers for their finest work but the popular resin-coated (RC) papers are much more convenient to use, and are preferable for most ordinary purposes. Both are really "paper" but the paper is sandwiched between very thin layers of plastic to make the RC base material. This plastic coating prevents the processing chemical solutions from saturating the paper base, which greatly reduces washing time, and saves a considerable quantity of water.

Test Strips

It's possible to determine print exposure times by using a special sort of exposure meter but it can also be done by making one or more *test strips*. These are simply strips of printing paper that sample a range of exposure times, so that after development the appropriate exposure can be determined by visual inspection of the image areas.

There are at least two ways to make useful test strips. The most common (arithmetic) method provides a series of exposure steps that increase progressively by some fixed value. For example, you might expose the entire strip for 6 seconds, then cover a part of it and give the remaining area another 2-second exposure. If you repeat this procedure for, say, 6 steps, the strip will contain exposures of 6, 8, 10, 12, 14, and 16 seconds, figure 14.7.

The second (geometric) method, which is most useful when you want to cover a wide range of possible times, provides exposures that double with each step. For example, if you plan a 6-step strip you might begin by exposing the entire strip for 2 seconds. Then cover a small section of the strip and *repeat the first exposure* to make the total on the remainder of this strip 4 seconds. Now proceed to make each succeeding exposure equivalent to the *accumulated total*. The next exposure is therefore, 4 seconds, followed by 8, 16, and 32. When you're through the individual steps will have received exposure times of 2, 4, 8, 16, 32, and 64 seconds—a range sufficient to include the proper exposure for almost any print under almost any conditions, figure 14.8.

After development (using either method, and assuming that the basic exposure estimate was a good one) you should be able to discern the 6 steps as separate image areas of increasing density. You may have to look closely at the arithmetic strip, however; the difference between 8 and 10 seconds, for example, may not be easily discernible, and the difference between 14 and 16 is insignificant.

If the image steps are too flat (gray) or too contrasty, change paper grades or filtration and make another test strip, figure 14.9. When you've produced a strip that appears to have satisfactory contrast, select the step that seems to show the best image quality and use that

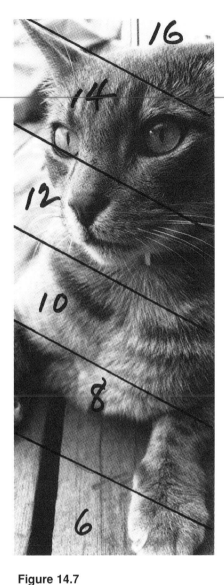

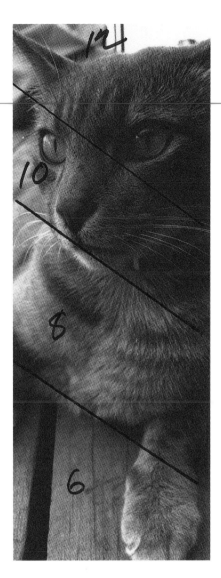

Figure 14.7
The individual steps of this arithmetic test strip (based on exposure increments of 2 seconds) were practically indistinguishable so their boundaries have been indicated with black lines. The steps would have been easier to identify—and more useful—if the time increment had been greater; that is, if the sequence had been 6, 9, 12, 15, for example, instead of 6, 8, 10, 12, 14, 16.

Figure 14.8
Geometric test strips maintain a more uniform separation between steps which makes the individual steps easier to identify. This is the best method to use when you haven't any idea what the proper exposure will be. When you've found the approximate exposure range with a geometric strip make an arithmetic strip to determine the exposure more precisely. This strip covers the range from 2 to 64 seconds and suggests that the exposure should be between 8 and 16 seconds.

Figure 14.9
The image contrast in these two test strips seemed high, so some yellow filtration (30Y) was dialed in on the enlarger color head, the lens aperture was opened one stop to compensate for the filter absorption, and this test strip was made with times of 6, 8, 10, and 12 seconds. The best time (with this larger aperture setting) appears to be about 8 seconds.

Figure 14.10
Test strips can only suggest the appropriate exposure and filtration. You'll almost always have to see the whole image to make final adjustments. This print, exposed for 8 seconds with 30Y filtration, is close but seems a little gray.

Figure 14.11
A 6-second exposure with 15Y filtration produced this image. Now the cat's fur and whiskers are brilliantly defined but because of the higher contrast the background is much too light. That indicates that this exposure is fine for the cat, but the background should receive more.

Figure 14.12
When you've reached a decision like this, it's a good idea to make a little sketch of the image (or use a scrap print), indicating the areas that should be dodged and burned. Also, estimate the amount of exposure that each area should receive. If there is a lot of burning and dodging to do it's probably wise to make separate test strips of each major area to establish the times accurately . Also, adjust the lens aperture as necessary to allow a basic exposure time of at least 10 seconds; it's very difficult to control the local exposure adjustments when the basic time is short.

Figure 14.13
Dodging and burning tools

exposure time to make a full-size print, figure 14.10. When that print has been developed and fixed, *rinse it thoroughly* to avoid dripping fixer, and inspect the image in the light.

If you're not satisfied with the quality of the image it's quite likely that either the print exposure or paper contrast—or both—need adjustment. One way to attack this problem is to adjust the exposure to produce satisfactory highlights (reduce exposure to lighten the print; increase exposure to darken it), then check the shadows to see if they're acceptable. If the highlights are good but the shadows are too light and gray, it means that you should choose a more contrasty paper (or filter). If the shadows are black without satisfactory detail or texture, the paper or filter contrast is too high and a "softer" (lower contrast) grade or filter should be selected. Remember changing papers or filters will almost certainly require a change in the print exposure so it's a good idea to make a new test strip and repeat this procedure until image density and contrast are satisfactory.

In many instances you'll find that the contrast of a *straight print* is satisfactory and the overall density is good, but some areas of the image seem too light or too dark (figure 14.11). You can often

Figure 14.14
In this case the lens was stopped down one stop so that all the times could be doubled, making the basic exposure 12 seconds. The cat's eye and whiskers were dodged for 2 seconds during the 12-second exposure, then the background areas were burned-in selectively to reach the total exposure times shown in the diagram. The final print preserves the crisp rendering of the cat's face and fur without sacrificing the background values. Notice the differences in overall tonality in the straight and adjusted prints. In addition to improving the detail rendering in the background, the added "burn" has helped to balance the composition by distributing the tones more uniformly. Of course composition is a matter of individual taste and not everyone will agree with this opinion.

correct these flaws by *dodging* to lighten a too-dark area, or *burning* (or *burning-in*) to darken an area that's too light, figure 14.12. If you want to lighten an edge or corner of the image you can use your hand as a dodging tool but if the area is inside the picture boundaries you'll have to make a special tool for the job, figure 14.13.

Similarly, if you need to darken an edge or corner you can shield the main portion of the image with your hand or an opaque card while providing the additional exposure. When you need to burn-in an interior area, cut a small hole of appropriate shape in an opaque card and direct the light that passes through the hole onto the selected area. If you've planned these adjustments well and executed them skillfully your final print should be satisfactory, figure 14.14.

Archival Processing

Although the print image is fairly stable, the silver particles that compose it can be degraded or tarnished in time by residual processing chemicals, by contact with various common materials, or by atmospheric gases. You can't control how your prints will be stored 100 years from now, but you can at least give them a good start toward long life by processing them carefully and washing them thoroughly.

If you want to prepare your prints for archival storage, begin by using fiber-base paper. Although RC papers are now considered to be very stable, that opinion is based on accelerated aging tests which may or may not be reliable. Fiber-based papers have been in use for almost as long as photography has existed, and their longevity—when properly treated and stored—is well-established.

Next, leave wide white borders around your print images. Image deterioration frequently begins at the edges of the paper sheet where contaminants can enter most easily; wide borders provide a "buffer zone" that can help protect the image from this edge contamination.

Don't prolong any of the chemical treatment steps unnecessarily and try, especially, to minimize the fixing time. Many fine art photographers now fix their prints for as little as 30 seconds in film-strength fixer, used without hardener. If the solution is fresh and the prints are agitated thoroughly and constantly while in it, this treatment is adequate for most papers and it has the distinct advantage of minimizing the amount of fixer that can be absorbed by the paper base. This, in turn, reduces the necessary washing time, and makes washing more efficient.

After fixing the prints you can improve the effectiveness of the wash even further by treating the prints in a washing aid or clearing bath. Many photographers like to tone the images at this point by adding 1 part of KODAK Selenium Toner concentrate to from 15 to 20 parts of KODAK Clearing Bath, prepared according to instructions. Selenium is a very poisonous material so it's advisable to wear protective gloves while you agitate the prints individually in this solution for 3 minutes or more.

This "protective toning" tends to increase the depth and richness of the deep black tones of the image, and may shift the image color slightly, but an additional purpose is to provide the silver image with extra protection from the possible destructive effects of external contaminants.

Finally, wash the toned prints thoroughly in running water for at least one-half hour, keeping them submerged and well-separated so that the flowing water can circulate around them freely. "Double-weight" prints and prints that have been allowed to soak in the fixing bath for more than a minute or two should be washed for an hour or more, if possible. Then squeegee the print surfaces lightly to remove water droplets and lay the prints facedown on clean drying screens to dry, figure 14.15 (plastic or Fiberglas window screens are fine for this). Store the thoroughly-dried prints in acid-free containers.

Figure 14.15
Drying cabinet with screens

CHAPTER 15

Finishing and Presenting
Your Prints

Los Angeles 1987.

Photograph by Brad Cole

Cole adds drama to these graffiti figures by
printing them in harsh contrast.

When your prints are dry inspect them carefully for white spots caused by dust or lint on the negative when it was printed. If you find any of these flaws they should be *spotted* before the print is displayed.

Every photographer seems to have his or her own method for spotting but most agree that the best material to use is one of the special commercially-available dyes, such as Spotone. Spotone comes in several tints that are designed to match the various subtle gray tints and shades that black-and-white papers can produce. You'll probably find that Spotone #3—considered to be a neutral black—will match the image tone of most popular papers quite satisfactorily. If necessary, it can be modified to match unusually cool or warm image tones by the addition of a little #1 (blue-black) or #2 (brown-black) dye.

Most photographers use very tiny (size 00 or even 000) brushes for spotting, apparently under the assumption that a small brush will permit more precise work than a larger one. I don't agree; a good-quality #4 red sable watercolor brush will form as fine a point as any smaller brush and has the additional virtue of being able to hold much more of the dye mixture. This has at least two related advantages: you can work longer without replenishing the dye; and that allows the dye to maintain a more uniform color and liquid consistency.

Also, small brushes tempt the user to think of spotting as if it were painting and as if the dye were a pigment that's supposed to cover up the spot as a surface layer. Actually, the dye should be *absorbed* so that there is no sign of it on the print surface. When this is the case—assuming that you've matched the image tone and touched the spots accurately—the retouched areas simply disappear and the dye becomes a semi-permanent part of the image itself.

Spotting is delicate work that requires good vision and a steady hand, as well as patience. Developing the necessary skill will take practice, but it will be time well-spent. The secret is to mix several small quantities of dye, from full strength to barely dirty water, and charge the brush *fully* with the selected tint each time you replenish it—don't just dip the brush tip into the dye pool or (worse) try to pick up dried dye powder with a dampened brush.

Begin by saturating the brush with the lightest dye tint, then stroke it surface-dry on paper toweling or tissues until, when touched to the print surface, it leaves no obvious wet spot, figure 15.1a. Then check the dye color by making a few tiny stipple marks on the print border. If necessary dilute the dye until the tone is barely visible against the white border area; then move into the lightest area of the print image and, with a cover sheet of paper under your hand to protect the print surface, touch the brush lightly to one of the spots using a gentle stippling stroke, figure 15.1b,c.

Work carefully, using just the tip hairs of the brush, and be patient. Increase the strength of the dye mixture gradually as you work toward the darker print areas but don't expect even the full-strength dye to obliterate a white spot in a very dark image area with just one application. It takes a little time for the dye to be absorbed so if you're working in a dark area of the print you'll probably have to let it "rest" after each few strokes. When you come back to the spot in a minute or two it will probably accept more dye and you can gradually build up the density to a satisfactory dark tone.

Figure 15.1a
Saturate the brush in the appropriate dye mixture and stroke it almost dry on tissue. Rotate it as you stroke to keep the point well formed.

Figure 15.1b
Greatly magnified view of a lint mark on a medium gray area of a moderately grainy image. Notice the fine brush point. A smaller brush will form no better point and will dry out much sooner, shifting the dye color and laying dry dye on the print surface. Some prints, especially those on RC paper, may refuse to absorb the dye properly causing it to remain on the surface as a granular film. When this happens, press the corner of a dampened blotter against the print surface in the area of the spot. In a few seconds the emulsion will probably accept the dye normally.

Figure 15.1c
Here the lint mark is partly spotted. Use a stipple stroke to match the grain texture and break the line into sections first to avoid the possibility of simply reinforcing the linear appearance if your technique is not perfect.

Figure 15.2a
Lay the print facedown on a clean surface and attach a sheet of dry-mount tissue to it with a light touch of the hot tacking iron. Tack it in only one spot, preferably near center.

Figure 15.2b
Trim off any tissue that extends beyond the edges of the print. It's easiest to do this if you take a narrow strip of the print margin with the tissue, but be careful not to cut into the image area. The mat-knife and straightedge technique shown here is generally more satisfactory than using a print trimming board or paper cutter. When using a mat-knife, *always* keep a sheet of heavy cardboard under the work to serve as a cutting surface. *Never* cut on an unprotected tabletop or desktop.

You probably won't become an expert print spotter immediately, but don't give up. Practice on old prints until you get the knack of it; then, when you feel fairly confident, go to work on your prize images.

Prints that you plan to exhibit should be *mounted* or *matted.* There are several ways to do this but it's conventional to *dry-mount* prints that you want to display but do not intend to mat. Matted prints may be either dry-mounted onto their backing board, or held in place with paper "corners" or "hinges" (see figure 15.5).

There are two types of *dry-mounting tissue.* Both are thermoplastic; that is, they soften and become adhesive when heated, then harden again when cool. I recommend the wax-impregnated type that is white, and feels leathery to the touch. It requires only moderate heat (around 180° F) and is safe for use with all types of photographic paper. The shellac-type tissue is usually brownish, relatively thin, and feels crisp. It should not be used with resin-coated papers because the higher temperature it requires (about 250° F) will warp or melt them.

In use, a sheet of dry-mount tissue is attached to the back of the print with a heated *tacking iron,* figure 15.2a; then, after the excess tissue has been trimmed off, figure 15.2b,c, the print is positioned on its mount board and placed into a heated *dry-mounting press,* figure 15.2d. In a few seconds the heat and pressure soften the tissue and stick the print and board together, and when the mounted print has been removed from the press and cooled, the bond is permanent.

If you're content to simply "flush-mount" the print you can now trim off the excess board and finish the cut edges in some way, figure 15.2e,f.

Figure 15.2c
Lift a corner of the print and tack the tissue to the mount board. Again, tack the tissue in only one spot to avoid creating folds or wrinkles in the tissue when it's pressed. The tissue that overhangs the mount board (right corner in the illustration) will have to be trimmed off before the board can be put into the press; otherwise it will stick to the press pad and make a mess.

Figure 15.2d
Cover the face of the print with a clean cover sheet and slip it into the press. Time will depend on the weight or thickness of the cover sheet and the mount board but from 10 to 20 seconds at 180° F is a good starting point.

Figure 15.2e
Trim the mounted print to finished size with mat-knife and straightedge. You can use a plastic triangle to keep the corners square and protect the print surface, as is shown here, but don't use it as a cutting guide; the plastic nicks easily.

Figure 15.2f
Smooth the edges of the trimmed print on both faces with fine sandpaper and a block. Stroke away from the print face to avoid chipping the edge of the image gelatin. Then wax the smoothed edges and polish them with tissue. You can use wax crayons if you want toned borders; paraffin will finish the edges without leaving any visible trace.

Figure 15.3a
Tack a piece of dry-mount tissue to the back of the print, then trim off any tissue that extends beyond the edges of the print. A print to be matted should not be trimmed to exact size before mounting but final image dimensions must be known. Determine the composition with L-shaped cardboard strips (cropping Ls) laid over the print. Then measure the image dimensions and jot them down.

Figure 15.3b
Determine the mat and mount board size by adding the desired margin widths to the print dimensions. Cut the mount board slightly smaller than the mat so the mat will cover it completely. Mark the image corner positions on the front of the mat board. Some mat boards will not tolerate erasure so make the marks as light and inconspicuous as possible.

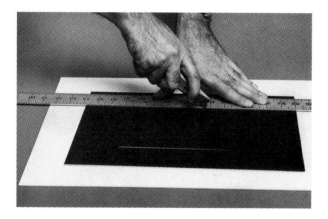

Figure 15.3c
Using a metal straightedge as a guide, cut the mat opening with a sharp mat-knife or utility knife. Always cut on the "waste" side of the straightedge so, if the knife wanders off line, it won't damage the mat itself. Cut just past the corner marks so the mat corners will be clean and free from tufts of uncut fibers.

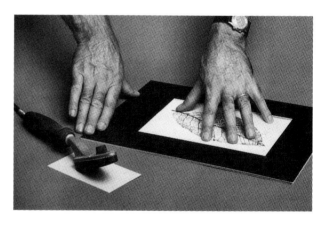

Figure 15.3d
Place the print on the mount board; place the mat board over it; and align the mat and mount boards carefully. Then slide the print into satisfactory position in the mat opening. Check to be sure the boards are still in exact alignment.

If you prefer to provide the print with a simple square-cut *over-mat* determine the dimensions of the composition, then cut matching mount and mat boards of appropriate size and proportions, figure 15.3a,b. Then mark the mat opening dimensions on the mount board and cut out the mat window with a sharp mat-knife and straightedge, figure 15.3c. Align the boards, center the print in the mat window, figure 15.3d, and tack it to the mount board with the tacking iron, figure 15.3e. Then protect the print with a clean cover sheet and put it into the mounting press to complete the bond, figure 15.3f.

Check to be sure the print is correctly positioned, then hinge the mat board to the mount board with tape, figure 15.3g, and the print is ready for display, figure 15.3h.

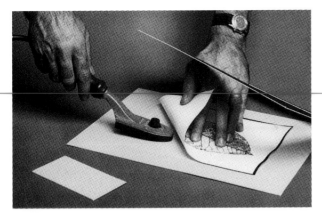

Figure 15.3e
Hold the print in position on the mount and lift the mat carefully. Then lifting a corner of the print, tack a corner of the dry-mount tissue to the mount board.

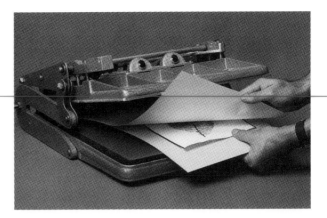

Figure 15.3f
Protecting the print face with a cover sheet, insert the mount board into the press and heat the print to bond it to the board.

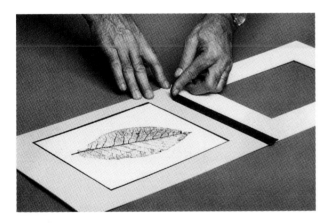

Figure 15.3g
Align the top edges of the mount and mat boards; the mount board should be faceup and the mat board facedown. Tape the intersection together to form a hinge. Use fabric library tape for archival quality prints, and plastic or paper tape for temporary use. Ordinary masking tape is not desirable; it will dry out and discolor with age and may damage the print if it comes into contact with it . You can, of course, dry-mount or glue the mount and mat together permanently if you want to.

Figure 15.3h
The finished print is neatly presented. Select mat boards in any color or texture that pleases you.

Figure 15.4a
Cutting beveled mats is not much different from cutting ordinary ones but a special mat-cutter makes the job easier. Here's one method using the familiar and relatively inexpensive Dexter mat-cutter. Determine the mat opening dimensions and mark them on the *back* of the mat board. You can be bold with these lines and draw them well past the corners.

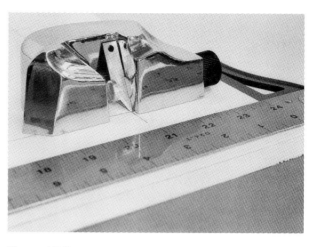

Figure 15.4b
Place the mat board facedown on a sheet of expendable cardboard to serve as a cutting surface, and align both boards with the edge of your work table or drawing board. This allows you to use a metal T-square to keep the lines straight and to use as a cutting guide. The T-square is much easier to hold steady than an ordinary straightedge. Align the edge of the mat-cutter with the drawn border line and insert the knife point just behind the cross line, as shown. Press it down firmly.

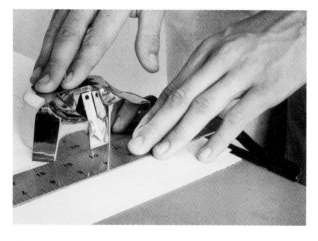

Figure 15.4c
Slide the T-square over to the cutter and allow it to square the cutter if it's slightly out of line. Check the board alignment again to be sure it is snug against the T of the T-square.

Figure 15.4d
The Dexter mat-cutter is a strictly right-handed instrument. Place your hand on it naturally, and holding the T-square down firmly, push the cutter along the metal guide. If the knife blade is in good shape, it should cut cleanly and easily without any tendency to wander away from the guide. Cut about 1/8-inch past the cross line to insure a clean corner. One authority suggests pinning the mat board down to help hold it in place—a good idea. Use a couple of pushpins in the waste center area of the board.

Beveled mats are prepared similarly except that the window opening is cut from the back of the mat board rather than the face, and a special mat cutting tool makes the job easier, figure 15.4a, b, c, d, e, f.

If you're preparing your prints for archival storage it's better to fasten them onto their mounts with acid-free paper corners or tissue hinges, figure 15.5a, b, c. These mounting methods don't flatten the prints as effectively as dry-mounting does but they do make it easier to remount the prints if necessary.

Figure 15.4e
A finished mat corner.

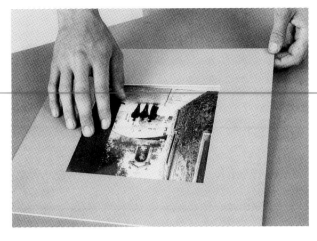

Figure 15.4f
Align mat and mount boards, as previously described, and center the print in the mat opening.

Figure 15.5a
There are several ways to make paper corners for archival print mounting. This is the one I prefer. Simply fold narrow strips of acid-free paper as shown and fasten them in place with strips of linen tape. I recommend *museum barrier* paper if you can find it (some art supply stores carry it). It's safe and substantial enough to make corners that will support prints of any size.

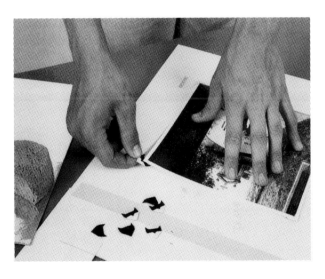

Figure 15.5b
Some people like to use gummed art corners for mounting. If you want to try this method, it's helpful to hinge the mat and mount boards before positioning the print. Then hold the print in position and open the mat. Moisten the gummed backs of the art corners, one at a time. Slip them over the print corners and press them down firmly. They stick almost immediately. I suggest using a dampened sponge instead of licking them (the glue tastes terrible).

Figure 15.5c
Some photographers prefer to attach strips of acid-free tissue to the backs of their prints, then attach the strips to the mount board so that the print simply hangs in place behind the overmat. Fold the tissue strips into hinges to mount small prints that will not be overmatted.

GLOSSARY

Aberrations Various inherent characteristics of simple lenses that degrade image quality in various ways; e.g., by reducing sharpness or distorting the format shape. The harmful effects of most aberrations are most obvious at maximum aperture and can be reduced by stopping down.

Agitation The process of stirring, swirling, or otherwise causing a liquid to move freely over the surfaces of film or paper during processing.

Anti-halation Describes the dark-colored dye backing layer that's intended to absorb light that passes completely through the film's emulsion, thus reducing the possibility that the light might be reflected back into the emulsion again with sufficient intensity to cause blurry halos to form around the image edges.

Aperture The lens opening; specifically, the circular opening in the lens' iris diaphragm that can be adjusted to control the intensity of the light that passes through the lens to the film.

Aperture priority The mode of semi-automatic camera operation that allows the operator to select the aperture setting, after which the camera automatically adjusts the shutter speed for correct exposure.

ASA Rating An old system for establing film speed ratings; it has now been superseded by the ISO (International Standards Orgnaization) standard.

Back light Light that strikes the subject from the side away from the camera, thus causing the subject to be seen in silhouette.

Baseboard The platform on which the enlarger column is mounted.

Beveled mat A mat whose window opening has been cut with a slanted blade so that the cut edge tapers slightly and serves as an attractive outline that helps to define the composition.

Block up To gain excessive density, and lose detail and contrast due to severe overexposure.

Body The camera "box" that includes the shutter mechanism, contains the film, and supports the lens.

Bracket To expose several frames of the same subject, typically overexposing some by one or two stops and underexposing some by one or two stops, in an attempt to include the optimum exposure in the series.

Burning (or Burning-in) During enlarging, the act of allowing projected image light to affect only a relatively small area of the printing paper for the purpose of increasing the local exposure; therefore rendering that area of the image darker than normal in the final print.

Cartridge The metal or plastic cassette that contains 35mm (and some smaller sizes of) film.

Center-weighted Describes an exposure meter whose sensitivity to light is greatest in the center area of its field.

Clearing bath A processing solution in which film or paper is treated following the fixing bath and which is intended to facilitate the removal of the fixing chemicals during a subsequent water wash.

Closeup A photograph, generally made at close range, that records the subject at about 1/4 size, or larger, on the negative.

Coated Refers to lenses whose surfaces have received a uniform, extremely thin deposit of certain transparent material that has the ability to reduce the intensity of light that's reflected from the glass, thus minimizing lens flare. Coated lens surfaces typically appear to have a magenta, green, or bronze tint.

Complements Colors that neutralize each other; e.g., a suitable blend of red and blue-green (cyan) light produces the neutral tone, white, while a similar mixture of cyan and magenta-yellow (red) pigments approaches black. The light primary colors are complements of the pigment primaries.

Condenser enlarger An enlarger that employs one or more large condensing lenses to concentrate light from the enlarger lamp and direct it through the negative toward the enlarger lens.

Contact Describes the arrangement of negative and sensitized paper as they are pressed together, emulsion to emulsion, in preparation for exposure.

Contact printing The process of producing a print image by exposing sensitized paper through a negative that is pressed tightly against the paper emulsion.

Contrast grades Numbers from 0 to 5 that are assigned to printing papers to identify their inherent contrast characteristics. See Graded papers.

Crop To reduce the size of the image by cutting off or masking portions of it in some way.

Cross light Light that is directed across the surface of the subject from the top or one side.

Dense negative A negative whose image appears unusually dark by transmitted light.

Density Darkness of a negative or print image due to heaviness of its image silver deposit.

Depth of field The distance between the nearest and farthest planes of acceptably sharp focus in the subject area.

Depth of field scale A calibrated scale, ring or chart—often part of the camera lens mount—on the which the depth of field for any distance and aperture setting is indicated.

Developer A water solution of certain chemicals that is used to transform the latent film or paper image into a visible one by chemically reducing the exposed halides to fine particles of metallic silver.

Diffusion enlarger An enlarger that illuminates the negative with diffused light.

Diopter An optometrist's term that describes the focal length of a lens as the reciprocal of the measured focal length in meters. For example, a positive lens whose focal length is about 20 inches (half a meter) would be identified as a "+2 diopter" lens. A negative lens of the same focal length would be labeled "-2."

Dodge To shield some portion of the printing paper from the projected image light during enlarging, for the purpose of reducing the exposure locally, thus lightening that area of the image in the finished print.

Dry-mount To weld a print to its mounting board with dry-mounting tissue, in a dry-mounting press.

Dry-mounting press An electrically heated device that is used to fasten prints to their mounting boards, using thermoplastic dry-mounting tissue as the adhesive. The print, tissue, and board are clamped firmly together and heated under pressure until the tissue fuses and bonds the print to the mount.

Dry-mounting tissue A thin paper impregnated with some adhesive substance, such as wax or shellac, that melts when heated and hardens again when cool.

EI number See Exposure Index.

Electronic flash A gas-filled glass tube that emits a very brief burst of intense light when activated by a pulse of high-voltage electricity.

Emulsion The mixture, principally of light-sensitive silver compounds suspended in gelatin, with which photographic films and papers are coated.

Enlargements Print images that are larger than the original negative image.

Enlarger A projector consisting essentially of an enclosed light source, a carrier or frame to hold the negative in position, and a lens that can project a focused image of the negative. In use the sensitized paper is held flat under the lens in an easel, and the image size is controlled by the projection distance.

Enlarger timer A timer that can be set to switch the enlarger light on at the touch of a button then, after a preset interval, switch off the light automatically. Most enlarger timers are electronic devices that can provide accurately-controlled exposure intervals of from 0.1 second to at least 99 seconds.

Enlarging easel A device designed to hold printing paper in position during projection printing. Most easels feature movable "blades" that can be adjusted to crop the image, if desired, and provide white borders around the image area.

Exposure The act or consequence of allowing light to affect a sensitized material such as photographic film or printing paper.

Exposure index (E.I.) A number that indicates the effective speed or sensitivity of a film as determined experimentally or by other unoffical means.

Exposure meter A device that can measure light intensity and calculate proper camera exposure for the film in use.

Extension tube A special tube that can be inserted between the camera body and the lens to effectively lengthen the focal distance so that the lens can be focused sharply on subjects at unusually close range.

f-number The relative aperture ratio rearranged to express the fact that the lens aperture (diameter) is equivalent to the lens focal length divided by the ratio number. For example, the relative aperture of a 1-inch diameter lens with a focal length of 4 inches, is 1:4; and the f-number is f/4. In other words, the aperture diameter (1) equals the focal length (4) divided by the ratio (4).

Fiber-base paper Printing paper whose base material is pure paper, as opposed to RC papers whose paper base is sheathed in plastic.

Filter factor A number that expresses the increase in exposure that's required when a filter is used over the camera lens. The numbers are simple multipliers that are most conveniently applied to the shutter speed. For example, if a filter factor of 3x is applied to a shutter speed of 1/30 second, the corrected exposure time is 3/30, or 1/10 second.

Fixing bath The solution of sodium or ammonium thiosulfate (principally) that follows the stop bath in film or paper processing, and is intended to dissolve the undeveloped silver compounds so that the negative or print emulsion will no longer be sensitive to light.

Flare Refers to nonimage light that affects the film in the camera. It can be caused by diffusion of image light by dirty or defective lens surfaces, by reflections between lens surfaces or from bright metal areas in the lens mount or from the inside surfaces of the camera body, or various other influences. The general effect is to increase image density and reduce contrast and, in severe cases, to superimpose streaks or patterns (ghosts) on the image.

Flat Low contrast gray; often used to describe a print image that is unpleasantly lacking in brilliance or tonal range.

Focal length The distance from an optical measuring point in the lens to the film plane when the object focused on is at infinity. The shortest distance between lens and film at which the lens can form a sharply focused image.

Focusing The act of adjusting the relative positions of the lens and the film (or viewfinder screen) so that some selected area of the image appears to be sharply defined.

Focusing aid Some optical device included in center of the viewfinder window that emphasizes the blur or softness of out-of-focus images to make the proper focus setting easier to recognize.

Fog (1) To expose film to non-image light, or to chemical action that contributes to the formation of nonimage silver deposits. (2) The visible or measurable silver density, not related to the image, that results from exposure to extraneous light or chemical action.

Footage scale A list of numbers, generally marked on the focusing ring of a lens and associated with a fixed index mark on the lens barrel. When any of these numbers is aligned with the index mark that number indicates the distance

in feet from the camera to the plane of sharpest focus. Many lenses provide scales that are marked in both feet and meters.

Frame A single exposure, or the film image produced by a single exposure. The individual negative images on a roll of film are sometimes referred to as 'frames,' and the speed of motor drives is sometimes rated in 'frames per second.'

Fresnel lens Typically a thin plastic sheet on which is molded a pattern of fine, circular, concentric ridges, which function as adjacent segments of a convex lens. Fresnel (pronounced 'fray-nell') lenses are often used in viewfinders to improve the overall brilliance of the viewed image.

Front light Light that strikes the subject from the direction of the camera.

Gradation The distribution or transition of tones in the image. Tonal scale.

Graded papers Printing papers whose fixed contrast characteristics are identified by number. In the usual range, grade #0 paper can be expected to produce very low contrast and grade #5 paper will produce very high contrast. Grade #2 is generally considered to be "normal."

Grain The granular or mealy appearance of the enlarged silver image due to the massing or clumping of the individual silver particles that compose the image.

Graininess The apparent granular texture of photographic image tones. Image "grain" is not usually visible in the negative or in small prints, but becomes more obvious as the image is enlarged.

Groundglass The matte or frosted glass or plastic screen upon which the viewfinder image is formed.

Halides Principally the silver salts of chlorine, bromine and iodine, which are the light-sensitive

materials used in the manufacture of photographic films and papers.

Hard High contrast.

Hard light Direct, undiffused light that produces sharply defined shadows.

Hyperfocal focusing Adjusting the focusing and aperture controls so that the far limit of the depth of field just reaches "infinity." This procedure provides the greatest depth of field that's possible at any given aperture.

Hypo Abbreviation of sodium hyposulphite which sodium thiosulfate was originally thought to be. Now occasionally used to refer to sodium thiosulfate itself, it's common water solution (with other ingredients) that's used as a fixing bath, or any other chemical solution that can function as a fixing bath.

Hypo clearing bath Same as Clearing bath.

Indicator stop bath A stop bath, such as the common dilution of acetic acid, to which a pH-sensitive yellow dye has been added. When the acid bath is neutralized the yellow dye changes to purple to indicate the bath's exhaustion.

Infinity Refers to the minimum subject distance beyond which a receding subject can travel—and remain in satisfactorily sharp focus without requiring further adjustment of the lens-to-film distance.

ISO The International Standards Organization. It has specified a method of testing and calibrating film speeds that supersedes the similar ASA (American Standards Association, now replaced by the ANSI, American National Standards Association) procedures.

ISO Range Any of the series of numbers now being assigned to printing papers to indicate their inherent contrast characteristic. ISO Range numbers supplement, and may eventually replace, the more conventional contrast grade numbers.

ISO speed A number assigned to each film type to indicate the film's sensitivity to light. Relative speeds can be determined by comparing the speed numbers; for example, a film of 400 speed is twice as "fast" (sensitive), and will require only half as much exposure, as a film rated at 200.

Latent Hidden, concealed, invisible.

Latitude The extent of exposure (or development) range within which a film or paper can produce an image of satisfactory quality.

Lens speed Refers to the relative ability of a lens to transmit light. Since the relative intensity of the light reaching the film depends mainly on the distance from lens to film (focal distance) and the area of the lens opening (aperture), the ratio of these factors, expressed as an f-number, is a useful indication of relative lens speed.

Light piping Describes the process by which light that enters the edge of the thin plastic film base, may be partially confined by repeated reflection from the plastic's internal surfaces so that it can travel for a considerable distance within the plastic material before dissipating.

Luminance The light that's reflected from (or emitted by, or transmitted through) the subject toward the camera. We perceive luminance as "brightness."

Macro lens A lens that has been corrected for optimum performance for closeup photography.

Macro-zoom lens A zoom lens that can be adjusted to function satisfactorily for closeup photography.

Mat The wide-bordered frame of paperboard that, when positioned over the print, serves to define the composition of the image and isolate it visually from its surroundings.

Matted Describes a print that is positioned in the cut-out opening in an overlaid sheet, or "mat," such as paper board, usually for display or presentation.

Medium-format camera Not a precise term but generally refers to cameras that use films larger than 35mm and smaller than 4" x 5".

Micro-prism grid A focusing aid consisting of an array of tiny plastic pyramids that refract the viewfinder image of an out-of-focus subject and cause it to shimmer visibly. When the lens is adjusted so that the shimmer is eliminated or minimized the camera is properly focused.

Motor drive A small motor, either built into the camera body or attached as an accessory, that winds the shutter and advances the film after each exposure, and can be set to provide automatic exposures at the rate of several per second.

Mounted Describes a print that has been fastened to a backing board of some sort, as for display.

Negative Any photographic image whose tones are reversed from those of the original, but specifically the developed film image.

Negative carrier The frame which supports and positions the negative in an enlarger.

Neutral density filter A colorless filter designed to absorb light of all colors more or less uniformly. ND filters are used primarily for exposure control.

One-shot Refers to a film developer that's intended to be used only once, then discarded.

Orthochromatic Describes films that are sensitive to ultraviolet, blue, and green, but not to red light. The abbreviation "ortho" is often included in the name of the film; e.g., "Commercial Ortho." There are no ortho films presently available for general use in the popular 35mm and rollfilm sizes.

Over-mat Another term for "mat"—the wide-bordered frame of paperboard that, when positioned over the print, serves to define the composition of the image and isolate it visually from its surroundings.

Override To deliberately change an exposure setting that the camera has selected. Most cameras provide a special calibrated dial or button for this purpose.

Panchromatic Describes films that are sensitized to respond to the entire visible spectrum—although not necessarily uniformly. The abbreviation, "Pan", is often included in the name of panchromatic films; e.g., "PanF" and "Panatomic."

Parallax error Describes the slight differences in perspective and spatial relationships between the film image formed by the camera lens and the image as it is seen in a separate viewfinder.

Polarizing filters Filters that are capable of restricting to essentially one plane the wave vibration of the light that passes through them.

Positive An image whose tones resemble those of the original subject; that is, light where the subject was light, and dark where it was dark.

Positive lens A lens that can focus light to form a real image.

Preview button The button or lever, provided on most SLR cameras, that allows the lens to be stopped down manually to its preset aperture so that the viewfinder image will indicate the approximate extent of the depth of field.

Print To expose paper through a negative, either by contact or projection. Also, the finished positive image on paper.

Printing filter A filter used to alter the color of the enlarger light for the purpose of adjusting the contrast of the image produced by special varible-contrast printing papers.

Printing frame An open frame equipped with a glass front and removable hinged back, in which negatives and paper can be held for contact printing.

Process The series of chemical steps necessary to produce a finished photographic image on either film or paper; also the act of producing such an image through a series of chemical treatments.

Programmed mode A form of automatic exposure control in which the camera's meter appraises the subject's light condition, then selects the optimum aperture and shutter settings.

Projection A printing method in which the image of a transilluminated negative is projected onto the sensitized surface of photographic paper.

Projection prints Prints made by projection under an enlarger.

Proofing The process of making quick reference prints from which certain images may be selected for more careful printing later.

Proofing frame Functionally similar to a printing frame, but usually simply a padded base equipped with a hinged plate glass front. Some proofing frames are equipped with guides that help to hold strips of negatives in place while they're being arranged on the paper surface.

Push processing Significantly extending film development time in an attempt to compensate for underexposure.

Rangefinder prism A focusing aid consisting of a pair of shallow circular plastic wedges positioned in the center of the viewfinder window so that they divide an out-of-focus image and displace its halves. When the lens is adjusted so that the image halves are joined again the camera is focused properly.

Reducing agent In photography, refers to the chemical ingredient of the developer solution that is responsible for converting the exposed silver halides in the film or paper emulsion into the particles of metallic silver that comprise the visible image.

Reel The plastic or metal spool onto which rollfilm is wound for processing in a small tank. Spiral tracks in the reel's flanges hold the film in position and keep the film layers separated to permit access to the processing liquids.

Relative aperture The diameter of the aperture opening relative to the lens focal length often expressed as a ratio, such as 1:5.6, when it appears engraved on the lens mount. More commonly it's expressed as an "f-number," such as f/5.6.

Replenish To add a calculated amount of concentrated chemical solution to a partially exhausted one for the purpose of restoring its strength and activity.

Resin-coated (RC) paper A popular type of printing paper produced by coating the sensitized emulsion on a waterproof base consisting of paper that has been laminated between thin sheets of protective plastic. Also sometimes called "resin-protected (RP)" paper.

Rollfilm Although, technically, all films that are supplied in rolls are "rollfilms," the term usually refers to the larger, unperforated sizes that, instead of being supplied in metal cartridges, are protected from light (while not in the camera) by an attached length of opaque paper. The popular 120 size is a common example.

Safelight Light of a color that will not affect a sensitized emulsion. Strictly speaking there is no "safelight" for panchromatic films, since they are sensitive to all colors. Papers, however, are not sensitive to the red region of the spectrum and can be handled quite freely in dim yellow-brown light.

Selective-contrast (SC) Another term for "variable-contrast," referring to printing papers.

Semi-automatic mode A form of exposure control in which the meter appraises the subject light condition, then expects the operator to select either the aperture or the shutter speed, after which the camera will set the other.

Semi-spot Describes a type of meter whose sensitivity is confined to a relatively small, well-defined area of the image field. Semi-

spot meters typically cover fields of from about 5°, to about 15°, as compared with the more specialized "spotmeters" that are designed to read fields of about 1°.

Sensitized materials Refers to the familiar light-sensitive films and papers that we use in photography.

Sharp Distinct, well-defined, not blurred.

Shutter The device that controls the duration of film exposure in the camera. It usually consists of thin metal leaves or blades that can be snapped open to allow image light to pass through to the film for the selected interval, then snapped closed again to terminate the exposure.

Shutter priority The semi-automatic exposure control mode in which the operator chooses the shutter speed and the camera automatically sets the appropriate aperture.

Shutter speed The time interval of film exposure as regulated by the shutter mechanism. The speed values are typically indicated on the shutter dial in seconds or fractions of seconds.

Single-lens reflex (SLR) A type of camera design in which the subject light enters the lens and is reflected up to the viewfinder window by an inclined mirror. When the shutter release is pressed the mirror flips up out of the way and the shutter opens to allow the subject light to reach the film.

SLR Single-lens reflex camera.

Small-format camera Not a precise term, but generally refers to cameras that use 35mm, or smaller, rollfilms.

Soft Low contrast.

Soft light Diffused light that casts indistinct shadows.

Spotted Refers to a print whose superficial blemishes have been concealed by careful hand work. Most spotting is done with water-soluble dyes and a fine-pointed brush, and involves painting out tiny lint or dust marks that appear as white marks on the print.

Stock solution A photographic chemical solution prepared in concentrated form to improve its keeping qualities or save storage space.

Stop (1) Refers to the lens f-number or aperture size (because the aperture "stops" some of the light from entering the camera), as "f/8 is a medium-speed stop." (2) Refers to an exposure factor of 2x. For example, increasing an exposure by one stop doubles it; decreasing an exposure by 2 stops divides it by 4. This use of the term refers most appropriately to changes of the aperture setting but we also commonly apply it to any influence that doubles or halves the exposure, such as variations in light intensity, variations in shutter speed, exposure changes due to filter factors, etc. (3) An abbreviated term for the weak acetic acid "stop bath" solution that is used in film and paper processing.

Stop bath The mild acid solution, typically about a 1% to 3% solution of acetic acid, that normally follows the developer in the conventional film or paper processing sequence. By neutralizing the alkaline developer it halts developing action and helps to preserve the following acid fixing bath.

Stop down To reduce the size of the lens aperture by closing the iris diaphragm.

Straight print A print made without manipulation.

Tacking iron A small, electrically heated tool that is used to temporarily attach a sheet of dry-mounting tissue to the back of a print or to a mount board, before inserting the print and board into a mounting press.

Taking lens The camera lens that forms the film image, as distinct from a "viewing lens" that is used in some cameras to provide the viewfinder image. In SLR cameras the camera lens forms both the film image and the viewfinder image.

Tank The plastic or metal container in which rollfilms are processed.

Telephoto converters An accessory lens designed to lengthen the effective focal length of the camera lens.

Telephoto lens Strictly speaking a lens of special construction that permits its physical length to be shorter than normal —in some instances actually shorter than its focal length. However it's now common to refer to any lens of longer-than-normal focal length as a "telephoto."

Test strip Any print that's subjected to one or more trial exposure intervals for the purpose of determining the correct exposure or paper contrast to be used in making a final print.

Thin negative A negative whose overall density is lower than normal and will therefore appear lighter than normal when viewed by transmitted light.

Time exposure Refers to any exposure interval that is timed manually instead of being governed by the mechanism or circuitry of the shutter itself. Usually interpreted to mean an exposure interval of greater than about 1 second.

Toner One of many chemical solutions that can be used to purposely alter the color of the print image. A few toners also improve the resistance of the print image to fading and discoloration.

Tongue The end of a 35mm film strip that protrudes from the cassette and is designed to fit into the slots in the hub of the camera's take-up spool during loading.

Variable-contrast papers A type of printing paper whose contrast characteristic can be varied by changing the color of the exposing light. Typically green light produces relatively low contrast and blue light produces higher contrast.

VC Abbreviation for variable contrast.

Viewfinder The optical unit, usually built into the camera body, through which the photographer can see the subject area that the camera will record. In single-lens reflex cameras the viewfinder image is formed on a groundglass screen by light reflected from an inclined mirror behind the camera lens.

Washing aid Another term for the hypo clearing bath.

Water spots Usually faint, dark, circular marks that form on film emulsion when residual drops of water prevent the emulsion from drying evenly.

Wetting bath A very weak water solution of some wetting agent that's used to reduce the surface tension of the final rinse water in film processing so that water droplets are less likely to remain on the film as it dries.

Wide-angle lens A lens of shorter-than-normal focal length, that's specially designed and constructed to include a wider expanse of the subject area than can be photographed with a normal lens.

Working solution A chemical solution of the proper strength for use in the processing sequence. Working solutions may be mixed directly from the basic chemical ingredients or they may be prepared just before use by suitably diluting a previously-prepared stock solution.

Zone focusing Adjusting the focusing and aperture controls so that the depth of field will most efficiently include some desired region in the subject space.

Zoom In specially designed lenses, an adjustment that alters the lens focal length, typically permitting it to be used as a "wide-angle" lens, a "telephoto" lens, or anything in between.

Zoom lens A lens whose focal length can be varied continuously over a substantial range without appreciably affecting the focus adjustment.

This Gray Card can be used with a
reflectance meter as a substitute for an incident meter.
(See Chapters 17–18, "Exposure and Development.")

It approximates an 18% gray scale.